THE

FAIRFAXES OF ENGLAND AND AMERICA

IN THE

Seventeenth and Eighteenth Centuries,

INCLUDING LETTERS FROM

AND TO

# HON. WILLIAM FAIRFAX,

PRESIDENT OF COUNCIL OF VIRGINIA,

AND HIS SONS

COL. GEORGE WILLIAM FAIRFAX AND REV. BRYAN, EIGHTH LORD FAIRFAX,

THE NEIGHBORS AND

FRIENDS OF GEORGE WASHINGTON.

BY

EDWARD D. NEILL,

AUTHOR OF "TERRA MARIÆ," "DAHKOTAH LAND AND DAHKOTAH LIFE," ETC., ETC.

ALBANY, N. Y.:
JOEL MUNSELL.
1868.

# PREFACE.

The name of Fairfax is closely connected with two of the most momentous uprisings of Englishmen, as well as with two of the most distinguished popular leaders.

Thomas, the third baron of Cameron, the hero of Naseby, is associated in history with Oliver Cromwell; and Thomas, the sixth Lord Fairfax, retiring to the wilds of the Shenandoah valley in Virginia, became the friend of George Washington, the successful defender of the liberties of Englishmen on American soil.

The following correspondence for the first time printed, it is hoped may prove interesting not only to the numerous descendants of the Fairfaxes on both sides of the Atlantic, but to students of Colonial American History.

E. D. N.

ANACOSTAN RIDGE,
    Near Washington, D. C.

PART FIRST.

CORRESPONDENCE

OF

THE FAIRFAXES

OF

ENGLAND.

# THE FAIRFAXES.

CORRESPONDENCE OF THE FAIRFAXES IN ENGLAND.

In the year 1822, some repairs having been made at Leeds Castle, England, a quantity of rubbish was sold, among which was an old oaken chest, apparently filled with Dutch tiles, which was purchased by a poor shoemaker from a neighboring village. Upon removing the tiles, he found beneath them several parchments and a number of letters.

Knowing no better use for the vellum he cut it into measuring strips, and the papers were carelessly scattered, some being used by the village mantua makers, as winders for thread. At length the attention of an intelligent gentleman was arrested, and he diligently sought out and purchased the scattered manuscripts, which were edited by George W. Johnson, barrister, and published in two octavo volumes, by Bentley of London, in 1848.

Not long since, a friend who had married one of the American Fairfaxes, told me that there was a quantity of manuscript in a trunk, at his house, which he would submit to my examination. One day he brought a tattered worm-eaten and mouse-nibbled bundle of old papers, difficult to arrange and more difficult to decipher.

From this has been rescued the following correspondence of the Fairfaxes of England, which, by a singular coincidence, proves to be a supplement of that which was in the old oaken chest of Leeds Castle.

Sir Thomas Fairfax, who purchased the baronetcy of Cameron for £1,500, was a solid, sensible man, loyal to his king, and humbly acknowledged obligation to his Creator.

In his youth he was captain of a company of troopers in the Low Countries; in the prime of life interested in agriculture and the raising of stock, and published a treatise on the horse; in his old age lived a retired life respected by his neighbors as a friend and counsellor, and wrote some devotional sentiments. After fourscore years he died in 1640, having had many children. Among others were Dorothy, the wife of Sir William Constable, and Ferdinando, the heir and successor to the title, who was a member of parliament at an early age, opposed to the usurpation of Charles, quick to buckle on the armor in defense of the liberties of England, and in command of the parliament forces at the famous battle of Marston Moor. This second Lord Fairfax had eight children, the first named after his grandfather Thomas, and known in history as the *hero of Naseby*, and the fifth was Frances, the wife of Sir Thomas, afterwards Lord Widdrington, the speaker of parliament, who administered the oath to Cromwell, as protector.

The correspondence which follows pertains to the marriage of Thomas, the third Lord Fairfax, to Ann, a daughter of Horatio Vere. Young Fairfax had served on the continent, under the brave and virtuous Lord Vere, the Chevalier Bayard of England.

The latter died in 1635, but his widow shared in the esteem of her husband for the then young Tom Fairfax and was willing that her daughter Ann should become his wife.

They were all religiously disposed, moderate but decided Presbyterians, equally opposed to the ritualism of Laud, and the irregularities of the Independents of that era.

The first letter of the collection is from Mary, Lady Vere, written in August 24th, 1636, to the wife of Sir William Constable, the aunt of the young Fairfax. Sir William was prominent as a member of parliament during the commonwealth, commanded a regiment, was governor of Gloucester, one of the judges of Charles the First, and signed his death warrant.

---

LADY VERE TO LADY CONSTABLE.

*To my honorable friend, the Lady Constable:*

Madam:

I cannot but take the first opportunity after my servant's return out of Holland, to give your ladyship notice of it as I promised that you may see I meant really as I spake and that my forbearing to treat then about the business was only because I knew not how my estate would fall out to be until his return.

The nobleness of your affections expressed to my Lord's family and my Lord's great affections and mine ever to yours makes me desirous to give you all respect and satisfaction which you shall ever find, and how truly I do esteem and respect your ladyship who shall ever have power to command

   Your Lad[s] most affectionate
      friend to serve you
        Mary Vere.
Stiskey, Aug. 24.

I shall desire y'r lad[s] answer of Sir Ferdinando Fairfax; his intention for I have not hearkened to any motion for my daughter, since it was made. I beseech you Madam, permit this to present my respective love to Sir W[m] Constable and my service to y'r Lad[s] niece.

---

Doctor Lawrence Wright of the Charter House, London, who writes the next letter, was a learned and popular physician, a correspondent and "loving cousin" of Governor Winthrop of Massachusetts, and an honored friend of Governor Hopkins of Connecticut.

DR. WRIGHT TO SIR WM. CONSTABLE.

*To my worthy friend, Sir William Constable:*

I understood by a line from my Lady Vere out of Norfolk, that according to her promise to your lady, so soon as her servant did return out of the Low Countries, she writ you, and which line did not only signify that now she was enabled to treat of a matter for her daughter (which she could not before) but also that she did willingly entertain the particular motion formerly made by yourself [torn]. She hath desired me to let you understand this matter and my request to you is that you will be pleased to let me know whether the motion made on the gentleman's part [torn] be pursued or not [torn] which I presume you will readily inform me of as she desireth by me you should understand her true meaning that no mistakes may beget imputation on either side but a fair and ready conclusion either way.

Y'r loving friend,<br>LAW: WRIGHT.

4 November, 1636.

Thomas Widdrington married Frances,[1] the sister of the young man whose marriage contract was being arranged. The letter was written to Lord Ferdinando Fairfax, and the Mary alluded to became the wife of Henry Arthington.

---

THOS. WIDDRINGTON TO FERD. FAIRFAX.

Sir:

I have received yours and the Judges letter. I could not but blush in reading the copy of the latter and return you humble thanks for all. I purpose to see Sir W. Belt to morrow morning and advise with him for my course and time of delivering this letter. I fear nothing but his being in bed for I must be early being necessitated by some occasions to be at Denton tomorrow night. If he fail of designating me a fitter, I must make use of cousin Wilkinson to whom I have already imparted the business. I must trust the success to the wise Disposer of all things.   \*   \*   \*   \*   I shall be much absent from home till the end of Tri-

---

[1] She died May 4, 1649.

nity term: if you would be pleased to let my sister Mary keep my wife company all or some part of the, you should do me a great favour. \* \* \* and shall ever remain,

  Y'r humble servant and
    affectionate Son in law,
        WIDDRINGTON.

YORK the 27th March, 1637.

---

The following, although without signature, is evidently a copy of one written by Ferdinando, Lord Fairfax, to Lady Vere:

LORD FAIRFAX TO LADY VERE.

Madam:

I understand by several letters from Sir W. that your Lad'ship demands the estatings of £2000 land by the year, out of which 600 by year jointure, and 500£ by year present maintenance.

The first with much more conveniency be yielded unto than the latter, which in these parts have not gone so high heretofore in any family that I can hear of what rank soever.

I must confess they are little enough for a daughter of your Ladyship, though much for them to give for those whose estates are not drawn up to a full value. Yet madam it is my intention to obey you in all things as if it please God the match speed. I shall subscribe to the conditions or anything else hereafter, which may concern the good of them.

I perceive likewise your Ladyship offers for portion £2000 at the time of marriage, and £2000 some time afterwards, or to estate land of a considerable value to descend after your Ladyship's death. To which I must answer, I know not what sum, or what manner of payment may best suit your La'ship's convenience, to which for my own part I refer both, being confident of your noble works and good affections to a well deserving child. Madam I have no more to say, but that I am

    Your Honor's most humble
      and ready servant.

My father has commanded me to present his service to your Ladyship and to signify his earnest desire to see a happy conclusion of this treaty.

The communication of Lady Vere to the grandfather of the suitor, indicates a speedy settlement of the preliminaries, and in a few weeks the nuptials were celebrated.

---

LADY VERE TO THOS. LORD WIDDRINGTON.

*For the Right Honorable, the Lord Fairfax.*

My Lord:

I know you have from Sir Ferdinando Fairfax, a full account of the proceedings of the business concerning my own son and my own daughter. I cannot let your servant go without this to say, something in it yet, notwithstanding some rubs in the way which Lawyers many times will needlessly put in. Yet now it is brought to that issue as I hope there will be no let to a good conclusion of it, so soon as a convenient time will permit.

My prayer and desire is, that as the Lord hath hitherto brought it on, so it will please him to give a happy conclusion by blessing it to us all and making her a blessing to your family, as I hope she shall be, for indeed God hath given you a great blessing in your Grandchild, whom I look upon with much affection: the match hath been with so much desire on all sides entertained that I trust we shall all have the comfort of it, which is the earnest desire of my heart and that you may long enjoy the happiness of it. And so commending it to God, I leave you to his protection, and will ever approve myself to be

Yo<sup>r</sup> L'p's<br>Most affectionate friend,<br>MARY VERE.

HACKNEY May 28, 1637.

---

On July 3d, 1638, Mary the daughter and heir of Thomas, third Lord Fairfax was born. She was married to George, the profligate Duke of Buckingham, on September 15, 1657, whom she survived, and, after a life of great trial, died near St. James, Westminster, October 20, 1704, poor but respected. She left no issue.

### BIOGRAPHICAL SKETCH OF THOMAS, THIRD BARON OF CAMERON.

*From the Manuscript of his Cousin, Bryan Fairfax.*

"Thomas Lord Fairfax was the son of Ferdinando Lord Fairfax and Mary Sheffield daughter of the Earl of Mulgrave. He was born at Denton in the west of Yorkshire, Anno 1611, Jan. 17th. He went into the Low Country wars 1627, where General Vere, baron of Tilbury took special notice of him, whose daughter and co-heir he married Anno 1637, and had issue Mary, Duchess of Bucks, and Elizabeth. He commanded the Yorkshire troop of Red Caps in the first Scotch war. He was knighted 1640, and was chosen General of the Parliament's army in the unhappy civil war 1645, and resigned his commission in 1650. He was signally instrumental in the restoration of his Majesty King Charles the 2nd declaring for General Monk then in Scotland (at his earnest request), against Lambert's army which pressed hard upon him as he lay at Coldstream, whither my Lord Fairfax sent me his cousin Bryan, with a verbal answer to his letter brought by Sir Thomas Clargis, that he would appear at the head of what forces he could raise in Yorkshire the first of January 16$\frac{59}{60}$; which he did to so good effect, that in three days time, the report of my Lord Fairfax's opposing them, being spread about Lambert's army, the Irish Brigade consisting of 1200 horse deserted him and sent to offer their service to my Lord Fairfax,[1] and several foot regiments at the same time declared for their old General Fairfax, and in 5 days time Lambert himself with ten men stole away from his own army.

"Then General Monk marched into England and offered the command of the army to my Lord Fairfax, but he refused; only advised him at his house at Appleton where Monk gave him a visit, to consider that there would be no

---

[1] "My Lord Fairfax was then at Arthington, with about 100 men, when an officer came and inquired for Mr. Bryan Fairfax (now Dr. F'f'x) to bring him to my Lord, with this kind and seasonable offer of their assistance."— *Manuscript note.*

peace in England until the Nation was settled upon the old foundation of Monarchy and King Charles the Second restored. And in the mean time to call the old secluded members into this Parliament, which had now got into their places again. The General was more reserved than he needed to have been upon this free discourse of my Lord Fairfax, being alone with him in his study, which gave my Lord occasion to suspect him ever after, until he declared himself the spring following that he was of the same mind, having received another letter at London from my Lord Fairfax, delivered by the same hand Bryan Fairfax, and accompanied with the address of all the gentlemen of Yorkshire for a free Parliament, and that they would pay no taxes till it met.

"King Charles himself did often acknowledge these services, not only by granting him a general pardon, but upon all occasions speaking kindly of him, and praising his great courage, his modesty, and his honesty.

"In the year 1660 he was one of the Deputies of that Parliament or Convention sent to King Charles at the Hague (where Bryan Fairfax went with him) to invite his Majesty over into England, where he was kindly received, his Majesty sending my Lord Gerard to compliment him particularly and to conduct him to the court, where he kissed his Majesty's hand. After his Majesty's restoration and coronation, my Lord Fairfax retired from London to his house at New Appleton near York (a house which he built a few years before) and where he peaceably spent the remainder of his life, between the pains of the gout and stone, with a courage and patience equal to that he had shown in the unhappy war. The wounds and fatigue of that war brought those diseases upon him whereof he writes a short account, which he calls a Memorial of his actions in the Northern War from the year 1642 to 1644, and something in his own vindication after he was General. The original is in Denton Library. The last seven years of his life that disease which he was most subject to, the gout, occasioned or increased by the heats and colds and loss of blood, the many wounds he got in the war, this disease took from him the use of his legs, and confined him to a chair, wherein he sat like an old Roman, his manly countenance striking love and reverence into all that beheld him, and yet mixed with so much modesty and meekness, as no figure of a mortal man ever represented more.

"Most of his time did he spend in religious duties, and much of the rest in reading good books, which he was qualified to do in all modern languages, as appears by those he hath writ and translated. Several volumes of his own handwriting are now in the study at Denton, with my brother Henry, Lord Fairfax.

"He died of a short sickness, a fever, at Appleton, November the 11th, 1671. The last morning of his life he called for a Bible, saying his eyes grew dim and read the 42d Psalm "As the hart panteth after the water brooks" etc.

"And so he quietly yielded up his soul to God in the 60th year of his age. His funeral sermon was preached by Mr. Richard Stratton, wherein he gives him his true character. He was buried at Billrough near York, where a decent monument is erected to his memory. His Lady was there buried also."

William Fairfax of Steeton, whose mother was a daughter of Lord Sheffield, and whose mother's sister was also the wife of his relative Ferdinando Fairfax, came back from the continent and joined the army of parliament, and was as brave as his relatives. In a skirmish at Montgomery Castle on November 20, 1644, he received eleven wounds, which proved fatal.

The Sir Wm. Sheffield mentioned in the letter was probably his mother's brother.

---

MR. WM. FAIRFAX TO MR. ROBERT BARWICK.

From NORMANDIE the
9 of December, 1640.

*For his much respected friend,*
  *Mr. Robert Barwicke, at his house in York.*

Sir:

Sir William Shefeild's man tells me that you refuse to pay the 500 pound you offered before the day of payment which will be due at Christmas. For my part had it not been your own offer I should not have expected it. I am sure I have performed all the conditions on my part, except Thomas Procter's lease, which I intreated you to stay till I came into Yorkshire, but since you will not trust me I have sent my man on purpose to see it done and to receive the money.

As for the dove coate I will repare itt as sonne as the season of the yeare will serve. I have sent you the fine. I know no more is to be done saveing my Lord Fairfax his release, and my sister's which I intend to gett at London very shortly. Bryan tells me you are troubled about a little parsell of land which belongs to Newton thatt lies within Toulston Land, for that I shall satisfy you, when I come to Yorke for I am sure it is nott in your reviculer, no more is the majesty of the law. Butt I will satisfy you fully when I come, till which time I rest

Your loveing freind and servantt
WILL: FAIRFAX.

The wife of Robert Barwick of Tolston, recorder of York, was a daughter of Walter Strickland of Boynton, and sister of Sir William Strickland, prominent during the protectorate. She was a woman of fine intellect and deep piety, recognized by all those who knew the truth of religion as an "elect lady."

Her son Robert, in whom so many hopes centered, and for whom his mother offered so many prayers, was drowned in 1666, in the prime of life. Her surviving child, Frances, married Henry, the fourth Lord Fairfax. Lady Barwick at the age of 81 died on October 4th, 1682.

---

URSULA BARWICKE TO HER SON ROBERT.

Roben:

The first thing I have to say is the Lord God bless and guide you in his ways, that you may make his laws your delight and meditate thereon day and night. I have often desired you to make the word of God your rule of all your actions in this life, and to read very much the proverbs of wise Solomon, for their is much wisdom to be had. Your happiness is very much of my comfort and contentment. I hope your being at Boynton with your best friends will be very comfortable to you, and such good company and society as that place doth afford, may be very much for your advantage, if you will have patience to stay there some time.

I know you will be welcome to them all and kindly used. I have sent you such necessaries as I think fit for you: if they may be acceptable and as well taken as I heartily mean them let me know what you want and I will supply you with whatever you will have. You have been too careless of your habit at home, I pray, be not so, when you are abroad. It is seemly for young men to be neat. I pray you to have a care of your health this sickly time, we cannot truly value that great blessing of health until we want it, and so the like of all other blessings we do enjoy. Roben I pray you be cheerful, and let our greatest frown be for our sins, that we do not live such lives as are pleasing to that great and most merciful God whose mercies never failed them that trusted in Him. Roben I do beg of God that he will be pleased to give you heavenly comforts, and then your life will be more comfortable, and then vain thoughts will not trouble you, and then you will be a happy man, and delight to be in good company, and godly society will be most pleasing unto you.

Solitariness is not good for you, nor will be any advantage to you, but do you very much harm, this is true and you will find it to be so. I will not trouble more at this time but to present my most humble service to brother Strickland, and my Lady Frances and my dear nephew Strickland. I bless God for his recovery. I hope God will please to bless him, and make him a strong pillar to uphold the house of Boynton. I do most heartily wish him all true happiness and comfort. I pray you to tell him what I say. My love to Mr. Rowe and thank him for all his kindness when he was at London. Roben the Lord bless and keep you now and ever.

Your affectionate truly loving mother<br>
to do you all the good I can.<br>
URSULA BARWICKE.

Henry, fourth Lord Fairfax, was the grandson of the first lord, and the son of the Rev. Henry Fairfax of Bolton Percy. His brother Bryan was a man of literary culture, the translator of the life of the distinguished Huguenot M. de Plessis. Bryan, son of Bryan, was the secretary of the archbishop of Canterbury. The amiable Thoresby in his diary mentions him as an honored friend and "a gentleman of great accomplishment and reading." His nephew Henry, son of Henry Lord Fairfax, became sheriff of Yorkshire, a post that had been filled by several of his ancestors.

Nathaniel Bladen, barrister, who had married Isabella, the daughter of William Fairfax of Steeton, urged the fourth Lord Fairfax to stand for parliament, as every protestant feared a popish plot.

NATHANIEL BLADEN TO HENRY, LORD FAIRFAX.

JAN'Y 25th, 1678.

My Lord:

It hath pleased the King to dissolve the Pl'm't[1] and to summon another against the sixth of March next, whereof I give your Lordship this early notice, that thereby you may take the opportunity of endearing yourself in a signal measure to the King and Country, by the representing your County in Pl'm't, a trust you will find them willing to confer on your Lordship for your own sake, as also for the performance your family hath given them on the like occasion.

And to encourage your Lordship's heart the more I give you the assurance of a noble Second (who can contribute no inconsiderable share of interest to carry on the joint concern) my Lord Treasurers[2] eldest son, my Lord Latimer.

My Lord, let not your modesty, or any other pretence of indisposition of health do yourself,

---

[1] This parliament had existed since 1661.
[2] Thomas Osborn, Earl of Danby.

your Country, your King that injury as to induce you to decline so noble a cause, at a time when the interest of King and Church calls for the assistance of men well principled in religion and loyalty. My Lord Treasurer hath applied to your Lordship (before all persons in the County, with the King's approbation, like an echo reverberated from those kind characters, wherewith his Lordship ever took occasion to represent you to his majesty) for an associate to his son, a favour which for the kind intention, ought not to be rejected.

But my Lord, if all I have said cannot prevail with your Lordship to appear on the public theatre, and that I have not reached some reasons which you think will excuse you to God, and your own conscience, if by your unwillingness to engage herein, you suffer a man to gain that point, who instead of balsam, shall cast vinegar into the wounds of Church and State and make the little scratches incurable ulcers. Then, let me beg of your Lordship (all arguments laid aside) to give your interest for my sake to my Lord Latimer, who will use that and all other of his own and my Lord

Treasurer's advantages to serve your Lordship and your family.

And this I beg for my own sake as presuming upon your Lordship's particular kindness to me, and I must tell your Lordship ingeniously, I serve a generous master, and that it may turn to account in my fortune. I will also put you in mind that it is still in his Lordship's power to serve the posterity of Col. Charles Fairfax.

I could wish your Lordship would also think of some borough where to cause my cousin, your son to be elected. I presume it may not be amiss to join interest with Sir Thomas Slingsby at Knarsburghe, but I leave the place to your thoughts, only wish the thing may not be omitted, for there is no school of improvement, for a young man of his quality, like the House of Commons.

My Lord I pray give me leave to insert my humble service to my Lady and pardon this trouble from

Your Lordship's
Most humble & obedient servant
NATHANIEL BLADEN.

That your Lordship may perceive that I do not desire to link you with a person your Lordship may be ashamed of, I thought good to enclose your Lordship the speech my Lord Treasurer made in the House of Lords to his accusations, than which nothing can show his Lordship better. And tho' Mr. Montague's endeavouring to take sanctuary in France by putting himself on board of a French shallop in a livery as servant to my Lady Harvy his sister's steward may declare his interest greater there,[1] yet I refer you to two of his own letters to make your judgment.

---

[1] Macaulay says, "The French court, which knew Danby to be its mortal enemy, artfully contrived to ruin him, by making him pass for its friend. Louis by the instrumentality of Ralph Montague, a faithless and shameless man, who had resided in France as minister from England, laid before the House of Commons proofs that the treasurer, had been concerned in an application made by the court of Whitehall, to the court of Versailles for a sum of money."

### BRYAN FAIRFAX TO HENRY FAIRFAX, ESQ.

LONDON, Oct. 30, 1683.

Dear Nephew:

I thank you for your kind letter and many other favours I rec'd from you in the country and visits at Appleton, and your welcoming us at Tolston. This kind disposition of yours to your friends shows you to be father's own son, and you will find respect accordingly especially from me, who rejoice to see you resemble the man I love above all others, and I thank God I may boast that the bond of brotherly love hath been kept inviolable between us, and I wish it may be the same between your brother and you. I am sure it will on your part by the respectful behavior I observe in you towards him. My wife is very sensible of your loving and kind behavior to her in the country, which makes sufficient amends for the want of it in others. Your old acquaintance my son Brian presents his service to you. We expect your brother at London to morrow. Let your father know that my lady Duchess is pretty well recovered, and she shall know how hardly he prayed for it.

Present my service to your father and mother, a letter now and then will be very acceptable, advise him not to walk alone for fear of his fits * * * * God have you in his protection.

Your ever loving uncle,
and humble serv't,
BR: FAIRFAX.

Mr. Henry Fairfax at Tolston near Tadcaster, Yorkshire.

---

Frances, a daughter of the fourth Lord Fairfax, fell in love with the Rev. Mr. Rymer the private chaplain. Her father, Lord Fairfax, was unwilling that the engagement should continue; but love conquers all things, and in time, she became the parson's wife.

HENRY, FOURTH LORD FAIRFAX, TO HIS SON HENRY.

June 5.

I would have you in my name to command my daughter Fr. as she ever expects my blessing or to see my face to forbear conversing with Mr. Rymer. He talks to me of a contract. I expect she should renounce it so far if it be one, as never to proceed further to marry him;

in this I expect as her father to be obeyed, and let me know her answer.

Y'r affectionate father<br>
HEN FAIRFAX.

Pray send her answer back by Mr. Banks immediately.

Mr. H. Fairfax at Tolston.

---

SHERIFF HENRY FAIRFAX TO HIS WIFE.

YORK, March 10, 168$\frac{4}{5}$.

My Dear:

I waited on your sisters last night, and heard Sir Will: Lowther intends to send his coach for them the week after the Assizes.

I've sent therefore to let you know it. I am returned upon the Grand Jury so that I cannot go with you myself to Preston but you may go when you please or come hither and go from hence with me, but it will be next week before I can be at liberty. My love to you and my sisters. Wishing you your healthes to be very merry this is all at present from

Y'r truly affect. husband<br>
H. F.

My lady Stapilton and Mr. Peebles are dead.

### LORD FAIRFAX'S RELEASE IN FAVOR OF HIS SON HENRY.

*To all persons to whom these presents shall come the Right Honourable Henry Lord Fairfax sends greeting.*

Whereas Henry Fairfax my younger son hath by my commission received several rents and other sums of money due to me, and I am satisfied with the account and disposal of the sum made by my said son.

Now know that I the said Lord Fairfax in consideration of said accounts have remised and released and by these presents do remise and release to the said young Fairfax my son, all actions, accounts, and demands whatsoever.

In witness whereof I have hereunto set my hand and seal this seventeen day of September, in the first year of the reign of our Sovereign Lord James the Second, by the grace of God of England, Scotland, France and Ireland, King, Defender of the Faith, Annoq: Dom 1685.

HEN. FAIRFAX.

Sealed and delivered in the presence of
    MICH. RYMER,
    JOHN BUXTON.

The fourth Lord Fairfax, the ancestor of the American family, proved a worthy son of the rector of Bolton Percy. Religion was always honored while he lived at Denton Hall. Thoresby in his diary, under date of June 8, 1684, writes: "Was much pleased yester-night with the good order observed in my Lordship's religious family, all which was called in and Mr. Clapham [the chaplain] read three or four psalms and a chapter or two out of the Old Testament, and as many out of the New, then after a psalm sung, prayed very seriously." He died in April, 1688, and a crowd of all classes followed his remains to the tomb, the poor of the neighborhood being sincere mourners.

He left two sons: Thomas, who succeeded to the title, and Henry.

Thomas, fifth Lord Fairfax, married Catharine Culpepper, the daughter of Lord Culpepper, who had been governor of Virginia.

Henry married Anna Harrison of South Cave, and in 1691 was high sheriff of York. His wife's sister, Eleanora, in 1689, married Henry Washington, a near relative of John and Lawrence, the emigrants to America. The seal used by Henry Washington bore the same coat of arms as that of General George Washington.

---

HENRY WASHINGTON TO HENRY FAIRFAX.

Oct. 23, 94.

Dear S$^r$:

On Monday night I had yours of the 16$^{th}$ and sure you think me guilty of a sham as you call it. I am glad you had so good a witness as one you call a friend to let you know it, but must beg the favour of you only to let me know his name which when done, if I do not prove him a lying rascal, then I'll be contented to wear the name of coward and villain while I live.    *    *    *    *

And since your friend that you style him though not worthy of the character that told you so great a lie, if you will not ask him why he imposed it on you, let me but know him and I'll ask him why he did on me, for never a son of a —— in England shall belie me with a design to make a misunderstanding betwixt me and my friend but I'll know his reason and use proper methods to convict him.

\* \* \* \* And if I cannot prove my disbursement then I am to blame but I can produce vouchers for it all. And I thank God my care and conduct were such, otherwise I guess how they would have been allowed. I ask your pardon for this digression. My wife's service and mine wait on you and my sister. And I am Sir,

Y'r suspected Bro. your<br>real friend & serv.<br>HEN: WASHINGTON.

---

Thomas, fifth Lord Fairfax, was a member of parliament in 1689, colonel of the Third Hussar Guards, brigadier general in 1701 and died in 1710. His wife was Catharine Culpepper. He was more extravagant than his predecessors. Denton, formerly the site of a nunnery, was much improved by Thomas the third lord. He built the stately mansion, with a gallery one hundred and fifty feet in length, and numerous rooms with mantel pieces of delicate and variegated marbles.

The fifth lord continued to improve, and in 1703 employed Gyles, the celebrated artist, who painted the window at University College, Oxford, to place in Denton Chapel the noblest painted glass then known in the north of England.

His expenditures exceeding his income, he became involved, and was much troubled by creditors. He died in London on January 6, 1710, and his servant who attended him robbed him of the little money he had left. The old Fairfax place now passed into the hands of strangers. Thoresby visited the spot in 1712, and says: " Was in company of old Robert Taite, who has seen the chapel and some remains of the nunnery, the old house pulled down, and a stately new one erected by Thomas, Lord Fairfax, the general, and now most of that pulled down, and a much more convenient though not quite so large erected by Mr. Milner. He remembers the first Thomas, Lord Fairfax, and his son Ferdinando, was servant to the third Lord, the general, and the Lord Henry and the last Lord Thomas were also survived by him, and he now lives in the sixth Lord Fairfax's time."

THOMAS, FIFTH LORD FAIRFAX, TO HIS BROTHER HENRY.

LONDON, Nov. 20, 1697.

Dear Brother:

I came to town last night and am going now to Kensington to wait on the King. I will do what I can to serve you. I will speak to the Duke of Devon, and will speak to the Lords of the Treasury but I know not what to think of ye matter since you are told they are likely to sink the office. I will raise money for you with all the speed I can, but Barradall drains me now, and the paym't I have had of the Treasury has been paper at nigh 40 per cent loss, such favour have I had. I wish with all my heart you had this, and if it continue I will use my poor interest. I cannot remember the particulars of my cosen Stapilton's disease, this in general I remember some thing of your acknowledging a debt to him one day and then when it was to be paid shuffled and disowned it. I cannot tell how but a very bad story it was, indeed I was ashamed, and uneasie at it and cannot now recollect what it was unless I heard him repeat it, which would not be very agreeable. I thought my cosen would not tell me a lye against you, and if it was true I could not tell to say in your excuse, but the non-paym't I am positive was not the chief matter of complaint. If I can have any hopeful prospect of your affair I will follow it with dilligence, and send you the best advice I can. But I am not like you with drawn cart horses (I own it) that will pull forever at large unmoveable oak. Pray give my humble service to all our friends, I am

Y'r affect. Brother,<br>
T. FAIRFAX.

Excuse haste, but I hope you may send my letter.

---

RALPH THORESBY, TO THOMAS, FIFTH LORD FAIRFAX.

My Lord:

I cannot forbear writing tho' the occasion be less grateful, but being yesternight in company of some of our magistrates, I was told that your Lordship not appearing 'twas verily tho't the Lord Irwyn and Sir John Kay would carry it the next election (which they seem to expect shortly). Tis certain my Lord Irwyn made the Corporation a visit on Saturday, and will doubtless have our vote, will your Lordship be pleased to signify your design in time, for tho' the country ought rather to court for the future, as well as thank your Lordship for what is past, yet as the world goes, notwithstanding the great services your Lordship has been so eminent for, there seems to be a necessity to let your friends know that your Lordship is willing to stand for the County. I humbly beg your Lordships pardon for this freedom, but I cannot bear that your truly ancient as well as right honorable family should be excluded, and besides the honor I bear to the family in general, your Lordship's special respects to me, has laid a peculiar obligation upon my Lord.

   Your Lordship's most obliged
     and most humble servt.
       RALPH THORESBY.

LEEDS, Sept. 9, 1701.

I shall be glad of the honor of a line, that I may have a pardon for this boldness, under your Lordship's own hand.

My service pray to the mayor and Mr. Bryan Fairfax.

Ralph Thoresby was the son of a Leeds merchant who during the civil wars had been an officer under the Fairfaxes. With his father he founded the once celebrated Thoresby Museum. He was a fine scholar, singular, conscientious and devout, a fellow of the Royal Society, and although a dissenter, among his friends and correspondents were some of the bishops of the established church. He published the *History of Leeds*, and at the age of 68 died October 10, 1725. Dunton, in the *Whipping Post*, says: "Ralph Thoresby F. R. S. is a very ingenious, sober gentleman and antiquary who hath a curious collection of natural and artificial rarities of many years standing. He is also a great preserver of manuscripts of all sorts. He is kind and respectful to his friends, and never better pleased than when they can present him with some piece of antiquity or valuable manuscript."

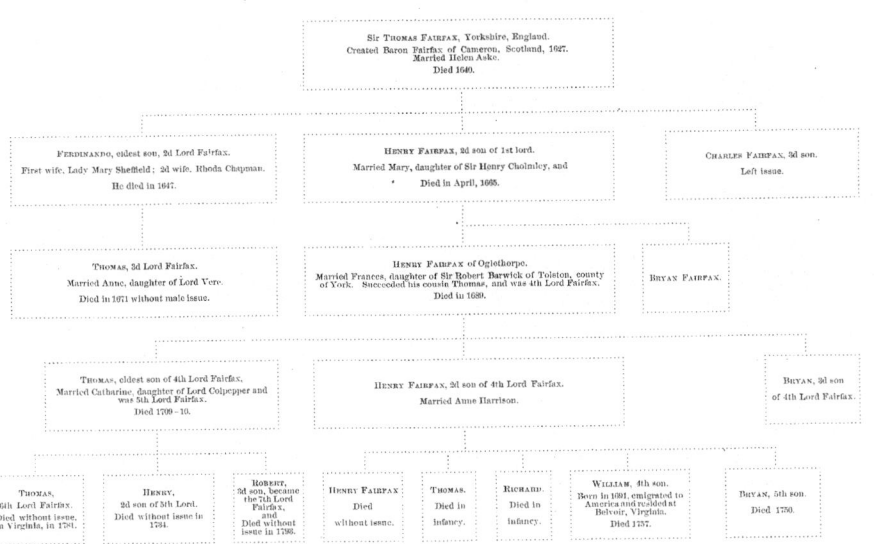

PEDIGREE OF THE FAIRFAX FAMILY OF VIRGINIA, UNITED STATES OF AMERICA.

PART SECOND.

THE

FAIRFAX FAMILY

IN

AMERICA.

# THE FAIRFAXES IN AMERICA.

### BIOGRAPHICAL NOTICE.

William Fairfax was the early and constant adviser, and his sons George William, and Bryan the youthful associates, and subsequent correspondents of him whose name is above every other name in America — George Washington.

Burk and Campbell in their histories of Virginia, erroneously state that William, the founder of the Fairfax family of Virginia, was the *son* instead of *cousin* of Thomas, Lord Fairfax, who lived in the valley of the Shenandoah, and was unmarried. The father of William was the Hon. Henry Fairfax, sheriff of Yorkshire, who was the son of the fourth Lord Fairfax. It has already been stated that his mother's name before marriage was Anna Harrison, a sister-in-law of one of the Washingtons of England.

His only brother Henry was well educated, but led a dissolute life, and died in England in

1759; William was born in 1691, and at an early age, was sent to the collegiate school established by Sir John Lowther, afterward Viscount Lonsdale; but through the influence of a relative, Capt. Fairfax of the Royal navy, went to sea when very young. Returning from this voyage he served in the British army in Spain, under Col. Martin Bladen, who had married a Fairfax. The letters written to his widowed mother indicate not only strong filial affection, but correct principles. For a time he was stationed at St. Helena, and subsequently at the Bahamas, where he married Sarah, a daughter of Major Walker, and was appointed chief justice of the island. About the year 1725 on account of the unhealthiness of the climate, he removed to New England, having received the appointment of collector of the customs at Salem and Marblehead. Here he was bereaved by the death of his wife in the year 1731, who left him four children.

Subsequently he married a Miss Deborah Clarke of Salem, an intimate friend of his first wife, who had expressed a wish on her death bed that she might be the step-mother of her children.

Thomas, the sixth Lord Fairfax, who became the proprietor of the northern neck of Virginia, through his mother, who was Catharine, daughter of Lord Culpepper, hearing that his agent was not faithful to his interests, invited his cousin William to leave New England and become the superintendent of his estates.

The offer in 1734 was accepted, and he at first took up his residence in Westmoreland county, but subsequently removed to a plantation called Belvoir, fourteen miles below Alexandria.

His daughter Anne by his first wife, married Lawrence Washington, who settled four miles above his father-in-law, and named his place Mount Vernon, in honor of the admiral with whom he had served while in the navy.

George, the brother of Lawrence, was thus at an early age brought under the influence of Mr. Fairfax, and on Sept. 10th, 1746, Lawrence Washington received a letter from his father-in-law relative to his brother, then fourteen years of age, in which he writes, "George has been with us, and says he will be steady, and thankfully follow your advice as his best friend. I gave him his mother's letter to deliver, with a caution not to show his." Mr. Fairfax had used his influence to obtain a position for George in the navy, but the mother would not consent to his going to sea, for "several persons told her it was a bad scheme."

Not long after this his uncle Joseph Ball, residing in England, wrote to his mother,[1] "I understand you are advised, and have some thoughts of putting your son to sea. I think he had better be put apprentice to a trade, for a common sailor before the mast has by no means the common liberty of the subject; for they will press him from a ship where he has fifty shillings a month, and make him take twenty-three, and cut and beat him like a negro, or rather like a dog. And as to any considerable promotion in the navy it is not to be expected, as there are always so many gaping for it here, who have influence, and he has none."

The year that it was proposed that George should go to sea, the eccentric bachelor Thomas, the sixth Lord Fairfax, made a second visit to Virginia, and remained there until his death at

---

[1] Meade.

Greenway Court in the Shenandoah valley a half century later; and under his directions William Fairfax in 1748 sends his son George William, a young man, and George Washington, then sixteen years of age, on a surveying tour in the upper part of the northern neck of Virginia. In a journal of this tour kept by Washington, he states, under date of April 12th, 1748: "Mr. Fairfax got safe home, and I to my brother's house, which concludes my journal."

Colonel William Fairfax was not only collector of his majesty's customs for the South Potomac, but after the death of Blair, president of the council of Virginia. At Great Meadows, in June, 1754, Washington named Queen Alequippa's son, Colonel Fairfax, in compliment to his valuable friend, and gave the young chief a medal. While he was there encamped Mr. Fairfax wrote to him: "I will not doubt you, having public prayers in the camp, especially when the Indian families are your guests, that they seeing your plain manner of worship, may have their curiosity excited to be informed why we do not use the ceremonies of the French."

On September 3d, 1757, William Fairfax died, and Virginia was deprived of the services of one of her most judicious councilors.

*His children by Sarah Walker, his first wife, were* George W., born in 1724.

Thomas of the British navy killed in action in East Indies, June 26, 1746.

Anne, wife of Lawrence Washington, and after his death married George Lee.

Sarah, wife of John Carlyle of Alexandria.

*His children by second wife, Deborah Clarke, were* Bryan, the eighth Lord Fairfax.

William, who died from wounds at the siege of Quebec.

Hannah, wife of Warner Washington.

# CORRESPONDENCE.

### HON. HENRY FAIRFAX TO HIS WIFE.

LOWTHER,[1] Sept. 24, 98.

Dear :

I were much to blame if I tell you our ways and weather was pleasant, for both were bad to a great degree yet arrived safely here yesterday, about two in the afternoon, finding my Lord, Lady and rest of friends in good health, and had a kind reception.

The first day we arrived at Caterick, the next at Appleby where I left Mrs. Lowther with her mother, who entertained us very hospitably. Major Lowther, my Lord's uncle sent for his two sons, and Mr. Kirk for his son to keep Henry company, so Mr. Kirk and I went

---

[1] Lowther was the seat of Sir John Lowther, who, in the year that this letter was written, became Viscount Lonsdale. His mansion was one of the most elegant of the age, and his library and paintings displayed refined taste. Interested in education he founded Lowther College. He died in 1700. In time the school was discontinued, and the building was used for a stocking factory.

with them to the colledge. Henry[1] liking his companions was very well contented to stay with them. Mr. T. Kirk is his bed fellow in a large room, in the middle story; in the same chamber is a large bed wherein Sir Matthew Pearson's three sons lie. There are about twenty-one or twenty-two young gentlemen, and six or seven more are shortly expected, so that the number my Lord intends to accept of will soon be complete.

I am sorry that my Godson omitted coming at this juncture if he is designed to come at all. Besides their school learning they are taught to sing psalms, and tomorrow will be the first time they are to sing in consort in the church provided the [torn] get their seat built. I hope Will, will make one of the chorus next Spring for the French master says, sooner the boys come the better provided they be in the grammar. Some are already come that be but ten years old, some about that age especially the Major's son, is as tall as Mr. Marshall of Newton and much thicker. I approve highly of every thing, and my Lord

---

[1] Elder brother of William Fairfax.

and Lady most of all, for they both join in encouraging the noble and generous undertaking.

As for my Lord's house I must not pretend to describe it at this time, neither my [torn] nor leisure will admit of it, so must conclude. Love, duty and service to yourself and children and friends.

This morning the weather seems to take up so I hope it may do the like with you that we may reap our harvest. The white Gelding's back being sadly galled is the worst disaster which befell us, mine not so bad, makes us think of staying here till Thursday or Friday next. We had some thoughts of being at Denton tomorrow sennight however. In so long a time we may alter our measures.

At an early period William Fairfax entered the navy, and on the eve of going on board the ship wrote the following affectionate letter to his brother Henry who was wayward and dissolute. The cousin Dick Washington spoken of, was the son of Henry Washington, who married Anna Harrison of South Cave, a sister of his mother.

WILLIAM FAIRFAX TO HIS BROTHER HENRY FAIRFAX.

MARCH the 3, 1709 – 10.

Dear Brother:

To what I should have imputed your silence I confess I knew not, for I could not apprehend how all your time was employed that one or two minutes could not be gained for one's service. But after this frank confession and earnest desire for remission I shall forget what's past.

Tho' our separation has been pretty long yet I in nowise despair of another greeting which I rather wish to be at Towlston, than any where else.

I am glad your's assures me of your innocence, as to what you have been charged with; tho' I must to justify myself, insist that I never too easily gave credit to any ill report of you, but the author who has been lately in town in my opinion would'nt have represented things worse than they really were; however if they were true I must impute it to the flush of youth, unwilling to be limited within narrow bounds. I would willingly inform you of my author, if

I could depend that your knowledge thereof were no other than to satisfy your curiosity.

I have shown yours to cousin Dick Washington who sends you his sentiments here.

You may with little entreaty engage me to answer yours, when my mind is so easily inclined thereto on its own accord. I earnestly wish you all happiness and pleasure. By this time you will hear of the arrival of your neighbour W. Hammond who set forward last Monday.

The next time you hear from me I believe will be from my ship, tho' I dont mention it as a precaution against your writing because I cant depend on the certainty of it. I am with unalterable affection,

Your endearing Brother<br>W. FAIRFAX.

---

LETTERS OF RICHARD WASHINGTON TO HENRY FAIRFAX.

FROM MRS. CROSIER'S, WESTMINSTER.

Dear boy:

As for Sir Robt. Berwick's deed of settlement I can assure you 'tis not in my custody. When our papers were brought from Lincoln's Inns I searched 'em for that purpose, but could not find any such paper amongst them. I will write to my mother about the pictures, and take care to send you 'em. My humble respects to my Aunt. All our news at present is the general rumour of peace, and the sentence of Dr. Sacheverell.[1] He is cast and to be sentenced for three years, his books to be burnt by the common hangman. I should be very proud to hear what execution hath been done among the foxes this season. I am Sir

Yr affectionate kinsman,<br>R. W.

---

[1] Henry Sacheverell, D.D., was born about 1672 and in college was a chum of Addison the poet. In two sensational and political sermons he advocated the *jure divino* view of church and state, which excited the whigs of parliament and caused his impeachment.

He was tried, and sentenced to be silenced for three years, and his obnoxious sermons to be burned. The Duchess of Marlborough called him "an ignorant and impudent incendiary." Bishop Burnet says: "He possessed little of religion, virtue, or good sense, but forced himself to preferment by railing at dissenters and low churchmen." He died in obscurity in 1724.

FROM MRS. CROSIER'S IN OLD PALACE,
WESTMINSTER, June 17, 1710.

Dear Harry:

I hope you will not impute my freedom to proceed from any disrespect being justly allowed to our affinity. But will rather favour this with such a friendly reception as may engage you to a return of these my first offers; for never having received any permission or countenance for a correspondence I have constrained myself till now. But lately reflecting on the obscurity and solitariness of a country retired life, I thought a friendly access by lines might not be at present unacceptable. 'Twould be a great satisfaction to me to hear how my countrymen divert themselves. What store of foxes, hares, stags, etc., you have killed last winter and what race was last run, and whose was the winning horse. In return I would acquaint you with all the news this populous town affords. At present we have a sort of pestilence amongst us. My late Secretary of State is turned out, who was my Lord Sunderland and my Lord Dartmouth put in his room. The Governor of Doway insisted on some unreasonable articles in the capitulation he sent to the Duke of Marlboro they were rejected. However we fancy by this 'tis surrendered. If you should see Mr. Hammond present my humble service. All here give their respects to Aunt and yourself. Pray accept mine & believe that I am with unalterable affection, Dear Harry.

Your affectionate kinsman [1]<br>
and humble servt.<br>
R. WASHINGTON.

---

[1] General Washington, in a letter to the Earl of Buchan says: "The family of Fairfax of which you speak, is also related to me. * * * What remains of the old stock are near neighbours to my estate at Mount Vernon."

Henry Fairfax, sheriff of Yorkshire, and Richard Washington, married sisters Anna and Eleanora Harrison, of South Cave. William, son of Henry Fairfax, became the proprietor of the estate adjoining Mount Vernon, and his daughter married Lawrence, the brother of General George Washington.

Richard Washington, the writer of this letter, was a first cousin and schoolmate of William Fairfax of Virginia, and in after years a resident of London, and correspondent of General Washington.

The Earl of Buchan was a connection of General Washington, David, 4th Earl of Buchan, having married Frances, daughter of Henry Fairfax of Hurst.

Mr. Chester of London, in *New England Genealogical Register*, has recently pointed out the error of Sparks in

CAPT. ROBERT FAIRFAX[1] R. N., TO MRS. ANN FAIRFAX.

Cousin :

I have yours of the 8th inst, and have sent up for your son, who I expect in town to-morrow, and have given his Captain the very letter which I got for him, so you will accordingly consider his equipment for his voyage being it will not be long consequently, before the ship will be going to sea; that he may lose no time for his advantage in the service of the Fleet I have been careful to obtain the letter, and I am glad to do him any service because he is a good boy and I am,

Your ready servant<br>Rob't Fairfax.

---

stating that Lawrence and John, sons of Lawrence Washington of Sulgrave, were the emigrants to Virginia. They were probably grandsons. Mr. Chester says that Richard, one of the sons of Lawrence of Sulgrave, went to London to live as an apprentice to a clothworker. Richard, the writer of the letter, may have been his grandson.

The wills of the emigrants John and Lawrence were made in Virginia, in 1675, and proved in 1677. John's second wife was then living. Lawrence bequeathed an estate in England to Mary a daughter by a former wife, and his lands and goods in Virginia, were divided between his second wife, and two children, John and Anna.

[1] Captain Fairfax rose to be Admiral of the Blue.

WILLIAM FAIRFAX TO HIS MOTHER.

Honored Madam:

I take occasion to acquaint you of my arrival in England and the receipt of your letter of the 7th of April, by which you was pleased to remit £5 for which I return you my filial acknowledgment. You was pleased to intimate in yours that you adjudged to my advantage as well as Capt. Fairfax my continuing abroad with Sir John Jennings.

I beg leave to acquaint you that I dont in the least question my Friends will think me in the right. When I received yours it was War, but now there being a cessation of arms, there are few Ships of War left abroad, consequently less vacancies happen, besides in a month's time, my Lord Forbes is designed to relieve Sr. Jno. Jennings, and so would only have drawn the time out a little longer. By a letter I lately saw from Sir G. Byng[1] in my behalf, I dare

---

[1] Sir G. Byng was born in 1663, and was an eminent officer of the British navy. By his successes in the Mediterranean in 1718, Spain was compelled to accede to the quadruple alliance.

be confident he will serve me at sea, if not I will consult with my friends about some thoughts I have of going with the Duke of Hamilton to France, when he goes as Embassador. I have been assured of his interest. This is the only time that I will importune my friends, and if all the interest and endeavours fail, I have resolved to seek my own fortune in some remote [end] of the world, where I dont in the least doubt of living better than I have hitherto done at Sea. I assure you I could wish my Bro. Brian would never settle his thoughts or have the least tendency to it. I have often wished that I had been a Parson, as in my childish years I began to fancy it, for they in all parts live the only happy lives, and without incident to those misfortunes, the laity often suffer under. By the time you receive this I hope to be in London, but where, there, I am yet uncertain. It would be an extraordinary service to me if you could spare me £30; I confess it is with regrets I am forced to make such a demand, but I dare to venture to assure you that if nothing offers, as I ought to expect it will be the last I shall draw from, being resolved to throw myself to Italy and France having this voyage learnt a little of the French tongue. Where I have so little title I begin to be weary of England. When I have finished what I have to do in London, I will take that so much wished for journey to Towlston to receive your blessing before I proceed further.

Y'r: most dutiful son & servt,<br>W. FAIRFAX.

December 12, 1712.

---

After returning from a voyage under his relative, Captain, afterwards Admiral Fairfax, he entered the army and served with Colonel Martin Bladen, the son of his relative Nathaniel Bladen.

---

WILLIAM FAIRFAX TO HIS MOTHER.

Hon'd Madam:

I have embrac'd several opportunities of writing to you since my being abroad, but amongst the number I only esteem those safe where the conveyance is not to be suspected. When friends and relatives meet in foreign parts their satisfaction is mutually exchang'd, and I think the kind fortune of presenting Cousin A. Lowther, has been very welcome for he is an officer well respected by his Captain and belov'd of his people.

As he has promised to wait on you in his way to or from Swillington, I refer to him the particulars of my present circumstance. The last news from England mentioned S'r George Byng and Col. Bladen[1] to be in great favour with the present ministry, insomuch that I intend with God's leave to make another trial of interest in England, as soon as I can possible. Pray present my love to brother and sisters, respects to all friends and relations.

    I am truly madam
      Y'r most dutiful son, and
        obliged servant,
          W. FAIRFAX.
St. Helena,
  Aug't 16, 1716.

---

[1] Col. Martin Bladen was the son of Nathaniel Bladen, barrister, and edited Cæsar's Commentaries. He became comptroller of the mint and one of the lords of trade.

Dear Madam:

I had the pleasure of receiving your letter dated in July 1716, the last June, therein I was sorry to observe that you advised my continuance at St. Helena, because you knew of no business I could immediately have at my arrival in England. But I must conclude that your reasons were altogether unknown with the knowledge of that Island. When I first received your's I had covenanted for my return, and as I in nowise doubt an employment more agreeable to my desires, so I hope in little time you will have the satisfaction to hear of my being settled. My Uncle Bladen sent your's enclosed in a very kind one of his own, and considering that he only of all those Gentlemen whom I have writ to did me the favour to return any, my obligation to him is the more encreased, especially when his concluded with a hearty wish of seeing me speedily at his house.

I am now on the road to London, when I shall hope in three or four days to hear of your welfare, as well as brothers and sisters to whom pray give my kind love, and to all friends.

My Uncle Bladen inform'd me of my Aunt Mary Fairfax's death, and of the kind legacy she left me. I received that intelligence as became a nephew, that condol'd the decease of my indulgent friend, and whatever suspicions might once have been surmis'd, I always thought myself highly favour'd of my Aunt and I trust in God I shall never procure the disesteem of any relation.

I am hon'd Madam<br>
Y'r very dutiful son<br>
and servant,<br>
W. FAIRFAX.

DEAL, Octob. 8, 1717.

LONDON, Jan'y 28, 1717 – 8.

Honour'd Madam:

My departure from you to-day recall'd to mind the time when I left you at Towlston, and the little outward show I had power only to demonstrate of that just concern might be expected. But I must beg you would do me the justice to believe, I have a heart fraught with as much sense of duty and gratitude, as the most open professor.

It is the strength of the conception which overflows my heart, and denys my tongue its expected utterance, therefore hope for your favourable construction.

My brother and I arriv'd in safety, and somewhat satisfied with our pleasant walk. My wife has since Saturday been very uneasy, because I sent her word, she might expect me then, which occasion'd her sending the messenger to enquire after me. Govern: Rogers call'd this morning expecting to see me, but told my wife that he had the satisfaction of having the ship return'd, which he sent to Providence, where she was, and on shewing the proclamation, and being acquainted that Captain Rogers was intended Governour, they unanimously rejoiced, and have sent their assurances of their hearty intention to accept of the offer'd pardon, also to compliment Gov: Rogers, whose character is not unknown to them. This is what I have learnt at present, and when I have seen Gov: Rogers to-morrow shall send a more particular account. My sister has got her cloaths, which had been stopt on the road by some Custom officer and examined on suspicion, and in a letter lately received from Towlston is desired to let you know that the mare Brian lost, is return'd home again.

My sister came this evening to pay my wife a visit, and joins with me, wife, and bearer in all duty. Love & respect to you, Uncle, Aunt, and Cousins.

I am hon'd Madam<br>
Y'r very dutiful son,<br>
W. FAIRFAX.

---

SHIP DELICIA AT THE NORE, April 19, 1718.

Honour'd Madam:

On Thursday I accompanied the Governour on board in order to settle for the preparing voyage, which hitherto has made but slow procedure, yet does not advance by quicker pace. I am pleased both with the Gentlemen, and accommodation on board, and believe I have procured so much of the Governour's favour, by my inclination to serve his affairs, that it must be own neglect, if at any time I shall want his assistance.

Indeed I never went on a voyage, but with hope to return with the ship, but my case differs at this time, yet shall never despair, (whilst I have either vigour or willing mind to advance my fortune) of both revisiting my native land, and again receiving your blessing with more settled purposes. There are many instances to be found of persons that have ventur'd abroad, and in a few years have return'd bless'd with a happy fraught of their labours, to the rejoicing of friends and self-satisfaction. * * * * * We shall be in the Downs in two or three days, wherefore I should be glad to hear from you before we sail thence, and hope you have had some remedies to relax your late ailings. Tho' I expect to be a little while separated from my wife, yet I trust in God, she will not want any thing to comfort her sorrows. She is indeed a stranger in England, known to few but my friends, and as I know she deserves a better fate than to be left almost disconsolate, yet I hope shall hear of the good intentions of some friends, that have been ready to acknowledge their zeal to serve her.

I do most sincerely, prompted by the mere

dictates of duty & inclination, wish you, Uncle, Aunt, and cousins all health and happiness, to whom severally I desire my remembrance and am Hon'd Madam.

Y'r very dutiful son<br>
and affection't servant<br>
W. FAIRFAX.

Mr. Graves is very complaisant to me with whom when we take a nipperkin, never fail of drinking to my Uncle's good health, as we shall continue to do.

---

MARY BLADEN TO MRS. ANN FAIRFAX.

SATTERDAY, March ye 30.

Madam:

I think it necessary to let you know that there is a Clargy man courts your Daughter, and indeed in all appearance is a very deserving young man, and is every way qualiffied for a Living, tho he has none as yet, but Mr. Bladen has promised me that he will do all he can to get him one either here or in IreLand. We both like his charicter, yet will inquire a little more into his circumstances, if you approve off the courtships going on, for my cosin Nancy I dare say will be obedient to all your commands.

     I am Madam
       Your humble servant,
         M. BLADEN.[1]

For Mrs. Fairfax at Tolston,
 near Tadcaster In Yorkshire.

---

### DOROTHY SHERARD TO HER NEPHEW.

Good Neve:

I return you my thanks for the favour of your letter. I thank God I am very well in helth tho I never ster out of my house all the winter. I am very sorry to heire my sister is in such a very ill steat of helth.

Pray tell her I have seent down the same sort of drops for her to take as I youst to seend her, and some Red Pills, and ruberb. I have desir'd my Brother to seend em to her, for theay are seent in a box to him and will be at Tadcaster, Saturday sennet for it is seent by

---

[1] Mary Bladen was the daughter of Col. Gibbs, who owned lands in Carolina.

York coach. I must now tell you of the good fortaine of my son Sherard, who by the deth of the leat Earle of Harborough, hee hes now that tittle, but the leat L'd hes bein soe good to him as to give him ye part of the Estate w'ch was his great Granfathers and ye other part of the Esteate is cheefly givern to the Duches of Rutland w'ch was his sister, and some part to my Lady Irwin's and her suns, but my sun having such a number of chilldren, it will require his good manneigment as much as ever to proveide for em in such a high stations.

I am glad I can tell you, all y'r relations o this side very well for most of em hes beein to see me. * * * I hartily wish you and my sister, and nece a [torn] and menny happy new yeirs, and I and my daughter [torn] humble serveis to you all and to my cousen Fairfaxes when you see them. I am

Yr: affect. Ante & servt<br>
D. SHERARD.[1]

---

[1] Dorothy, daughter of Henry Lord Fairfax, first married R. Stapleton. After his death she became the wife of Bennet Sherard, and her son became Earl of Harborough. She died in 1744.

The ship Delicia arrived at Nassau, New Providence, in July, 1718, and Woodes Rogers, distinguished for a three years' voyage around the world, who had been sènt out on petition of the Liverpool merchants to break up the nest of pirates there, immediately entered upon his duties as governor. William Fairfax was appointed judge of the Admiralty, and acted as president of the court, which in December tried, found guilty, and hung a number of desperadoes.

Owing to the sickliness of the climate, in 1725 he moved to New England, where his wife, the daughter of Major Walker of Nassau, died in 1731.

HON. WM. FAIRFAX TO HIS MOTHER.

CUSTOM HOUSE, SALEM [1]
IN NEW ENGLAND, 24 May, 1731.

Ever honoured Madam:

I have once again the great pleasure to write by Col'o Gale who in his way for England has paid me a visit, well knowing that the opportunity would be most agreeable. His long and

---

[1] In 1734 he left Salem for Virginia. See Felt's *Salem*.

continued acquaintance with my affairs, and my now present circumstances will make it unnecessary to repeat the former account I have given you of the decease of my dear Dame on the 18th of January last, and her having left me four small children. Col° Gale has indeed kindly offered to take the care of safe conducting my eldest son George, upwards of seven years old, but I judged it too forward to send him before I had your's or some one of his Uncles' or Aunts' invitation, altho' I have no reason to doubt any of their indulgences to poor West India boy * * * * * I and mine are with all duty, love and respect humble petitioners that you will please to continue your prayers to God for a blessing on our endeavours to live happily here and hereafter. I am most dutiful mother,

Your ever dutiful son and servant
W. FAIRFAX.

In 1750 Mr. Fairfax visited England, where his son William Henry was probably at the Blue Coat school of Beverley in Yorkshire.

HON. WM. FAIRFAX, TO A BROTHER.

BEVERLEY, 28th Sept$^r$. 1750.

Sir:

I have had the pleasure to find Col. Beverley, his family, and my son William Henry in good health.

On discoursing with Mr. Clarke the worthy school master, I find that several of the books under Wm. Appleyard's care will be useful to my son, therefore take the freedom to entreat your favor to receive and forward the books to be sent you. If there be any books that please and worth your acceptance I shall be glad if you will take them. Mrs. Beverley and family send their best compliments and I hope you will favor me with your good correspondence, while I am in London which will be always agreeable to

Yr very affect. brother, &c.

W. FAIRFAX.

---

Thomas, the sixth Lord Fairfax, whose mother was a daughter of Lord Culpepper, owned a vast estate in the northern neck of

Virginia; and discovering neglect upon the part of his mother's agent, he dismissed him, and, as has been stated, appointed his cousin, Colonel William Fairfax.

Colonel Fairfax upon his first removal from New England to Virginia lived in Westmoreland, but afterwards moved to the banks of the Potomac, and built Belvoir, a pleasant residence, in sight of what is now called Mt. Vernon.

Lord Fairfax first visited Virginia in 1736, and passed a year with his cousin. A graduate of Oxford, and possessed of literary taste, partly owing to disappointed affection he sought the Virginia wilderness, and shunned the conventionalities of society. In the year 1746 he made Virginia his permanent residence, and the letter from Leeds Castle to his cousin George, the son of Colonel William Fairfax, was probably written just before his final departure from England.

THOS. LORD FAIRFAX TO GEO. W. FAIRFAX.

LEEDS CASTLE, April 6.

Dear George:

I here send you by Captain Cooling of the Elizabeth, two dogs and one bitch of S$^r$ Edward Filmores hounds which he promised you. I desire you will be very careful of them and get into the breed; if you have any other good hounds they will make a good cross and mend the breeds. If there is any charge attending them I have wrote to your father to satisfy Captain Cooling. I do not yet hear of any convoy appointed for Virginia, but I hope soon to know of one being named that I may soon have the pleasure of seeing my friends in the Northern Neck. I hope likewise soon of having the pleasure of acquainting you of something to your advantage. The Major desires his compliments and reminds you of his turkeys. I have nothing more to add at present but that I remain

       Yours
         FAIRFAX.

---

LORD FAIRFAX TO GEO. W. FAIRFAX.

    FREDERICK, October 28, 1751.

Sir:

I have promised Mr. John West to lend him one hundred pounds sterling w'ch you may pay him and take his bond for. There are two steers and one cow of mine at Potter's, if they will be of any service to you, you may send for them before Potter leaves your parts.

My service attends all the good family, as also Mr. Martins. I remain

Yours
FAIRFAX.

---

LORD FAIRFAX TO HON. WM. FAIRFAX.

Sir:

Yours I received from Williamsburg by which I was glad to hear of all the good Family's health. We have no news in this part of the world. We have had hitherto very fine weather, but now it begins to be very cold, and likely to set in for wet weather. Two or three days ago we had a small snow but it soon melted. Please to let Mr. Lewis[1] have his own and any of his neighbours deeds out of the office. His note is as good as cash as there is an account between

---

[1] John Lewis of Ireland was the first settler of Augusta county, and founder of the town of Staunton. He died in 1762, aged eighty-four. He left five sons: Thomas, a man of learning and integrity, and a member of the convention of 1776; Samuel; General Andrew; William, an officer in the army of the revolution; and Colonel Charles.

Thomas is probably the one alluded to in the note.

him and me, which you may at any time send up to me. My service attends Col. George, Mrs. Fairfax and all friends. I remain

Dear cousin<br>Yours<br>FAIRFAX.

---

GEORGE W. FAIRFAX TO GOVERNOR DINWIDDIE, OF VIRGINIA.

WINCHESTER, Sept'r 4th, 1755.

Hon<sup>ble</sup> Sir:

This instant Mr. Dennis McCarty[1] came here and gave me the agreeable news of Col. Dunbar's[2] being ordered back, and that my friend Col. Washington is to have command of the forces to be raised by this Colony, which undoubtedly is a great trust, but I dare say he will discharge it with honour. I could wish our good Countrymen were not so tenacious of their liber-

---

[1] Early in the eighteenth century, Daniel McCarty, the ancestor of Dennis came to Westmoreland county, Va., and was speaker of the house of burgesses in 1715. Dennis was appointed a captain by Washington. Mr. McCarty and family were at Mrs. Washington's request present at her husband's funeral.

[2] Dunbar was colonel of the 48th regiment British Regulars, and was the senior officer after Braddock's defeat and death at Fort Duquesne, the previous July.

ties at this time, and put the Soldiery during the expedition under martial law, and then I am sure he would do it with great satisfaction, and engage others to enter into the service. I can't help expressing my intention, and great desire of serving my Country at this juncture, if you should be at a loss for officers, not sembling in the least to serve under my valuable friend. Had I the least reason to expect this when I last saw him, I should have mentioned it and wrote to your Honour, but I hope I am not too late in my application, and must beg the favour of you to postpone any office you may incline to favour me with till I consult my good and indulgent Parent, and my worthy Patron L'd Fairfax who I am in hopes will spare me from his office. . Wives, good Sir, are not to be consulted upon these occasions, but I make no doubt but mine would consent upon so laudable a call.[1]

I tarried but one day at home, before I set off for this County in which I have been endeavouring ever since to get men for the companies of rangers and I am sorry to say with

---

[1] His wife was Sarah, the daughter of Wilson Cary.

but little success, but what we have, being about — I think are good, expert, active woodsmen such as I do intend to and can trust myself with, and do propose to march them on next Saturday if possible, and to leave Capt. Cocke to bring up the remainder of his rangers, and some of his militia troops which his Lordship and we think most expeditious and necessary for the defence of the back inhabitants until further orders. For at our general muster, we drafted pursuant to the Act made for that purpose 30 young men, out of which we could not get one to enlist, or pay the Ten pounds. Upon which we committed the whole to prison, where I set a good and efficient guard every night, and yesterday about twelve oClock the prisoners artfully or by some assistance put the lock back, and took an opportunity of rushing out in a body with clubs, and through the guard, and have all made their escape, notwithstanding we sent several horsemen after them, and was kindly assisted by Capt. Stuart's horse.

Thus good Sir I have been perplexed, and am at a loss what to do indeed with those that are enlisted in case they should misbehave. I should have wrote by Mr. McCarty but he would not tarry and now am hurried to take this opportunity. Please to present my kind compliments to your good Lady and family, and be assured that I am with the greatest esteem

Your honour's most ob't humble servant

GEO. WM. FAIRFAX.

---

LORD FAIRFAX TO GEORGE W. FAIRFAX.

Thursday Evening.

Dear George:

I was yesterday down at Mr. West's on my way to Belvoir, but was called back by a false alarm of old Sharpe's[1] of which I wrote an account to Mr. Carlyle;[2] tho' the first part, namely the twenty men being either killed or taken is true. I propose setting off once more by the way of Prince W$^m$. as we now imagine the Indians are for the present gone back. I have no objection to what you mention in your letter if you think it will any ways to your advantage. I have nothing farther to add till I

[1] Governor Sharpe of Maryland was very unpopular with the Virginians.
[2] Mr. Carlyle married the sister of George Fairfax.

shall have the pleasure of seeing you. My service attends Mrs. Fairfax and the rest of the family.

I remain Yours<br>FAIRFAX.

---

LORD FAIRFAX TO GEO. W. FAIRFAX.

May 5, 1756.

Dear George:

I wrote to you some time ago about a piece of land surveyed for Ben Smith on Opeckon, who married Captain Chester's[1] daughter, who has been with me, and has given her consent that the deed should come out in the name of Mr. John Hogg.[2] The said Smith has run away to Carolina, and she for the benefit of her

---

[1] Capt. Chester was an early settler in the valley of the Shenandoah. Fothergill, a quaker preacher, brother of the distinguished English physician, says in his journal, under date of 9th mo. 13th. 1736:

"We got over Shenandoah river to one Chester's who was very courteous to us, his poor circumstances considered."

[2] The Hoge family came to Frederick county in 1738. George Hoge was one of the first justices of the court. John Hoge, perhaps son of George, graduated at Princeton, in 1748. William, a relative of George, was a native of Paisley, Scotland, and after a brief residence in the middle states, settled near Winchester. Moses, one of his sons, became a professor of theology.

children has agreed with the said Hog and the executors of Capt. Chester to exchange said land for another of Chester's whereon she has always lived. If it is agreeable to the practice of the office, I am willing to consent to it, and will take care that the children have justice done them by Chester's executors.

I remain Yours<br>
FAIRFAX.

H. CLAPHAM TO HON. WILLIAM FAIRFAX.

HULL, 1st March, 1757.

D<sup>r</sup> S<sup>r</sup>:

It's now above a year, since we have had any letters from Virginia, two of our ships, viz Capt. Cheeseman and Capt. Lewis, by both of whom we wrote, being taken by French privateers, upon our own Coasts. This comes by Capt. Cheeseman who ransomed his ship and cargo for £1000 the cargo belonging to Mr. Welfil.

As to affairs here we are in the utmost confusion, the Ministry being entirely changed, and Bing who behaved so ill in the Mediterranean, I believe if one may credit the papers was to be shot on board the 'Royal Anne at

Spithead on yesterday.[1] The greatest preparations for war are making that was ever known in the memory of man, the whole Nation being united to humble the French, and want only good commanders that will fight. I am with mine and my wife's best respects to yourself, family, and all friends in Virginia,

Yr: affect. brother<br>and humble Serv't<br>H. CLAPHAM.

---

DOROTHY CLAPHAM TO HER BROTHER HON. WM. FAIRFAX.

Dear Brother:

I have been troubled very much by not hearing from you so long, and we have sent you many letters, and as Captain Cheesman told Mr. Clapham[2] he had a packet for us, but when he found he should be taken he threw all over into the sea. I got a letter lately from my poor Willy who writes from London. The last

---

[1] John Byng, son of Viscount Torrington, was tried for alleged cowardice and unjustly executed. He was shot at Portsmouth, and met his sad fate like a man and Christian.

[2] H. Clapham was an officer of the customs in England, and Dorothy, his wife, was sister of William Fairfax of Belvoir, Va.

time I saw him was last year at York. He is tall and good-like, God bless him and send him grace. We drunk tea together with my brother for I had not gone to York, but word was sent to us that he was very ill so stayed till he was better and so went to Newton, and dined one day there, and lay two nights at William Appleyards, and two at the More House * * * * went to see the Hall, it made my heart ache to see so ruined a place. I am dear brother

Your loving sister & humble servant

DOROTHY CLAPHAM.

---

JOHN HOGE, PRISONER OF WAR, COGNAC, FRANCE, TO LORD FAIRFAX.

COGNAC, March 27, 1757.

Lord Thomas Fairfax:

Sir:

I make bold to write you a few lines to let you know of my being a prisoner in old France, and should be glad if you would forward it to my father, as I am well assured he dont think of my being in the land of the living, and the condition I am now in, makes me rely upon [torn] some relief, being in great want of the necessary [torn] having the second shirt or jacket to put to my [torn] of all I had, when I was taken by the Indians and [torn] Royal, and from there was sent to this prison. [torn] remain having no likelihood or hopes of being [torn] I understand there is a dispute between both [torn] Prisoners that were taken before the war was dec [torn] ever relief my father is pleased to send me by the way of Lond [torn] correspondence in England, and that your Lordship [torn] me to them, to befriend me in the way of getting [torn] in his majesty's service, which if your Lordship [torn] I shall always think myself highly obligated to your Honour for doing so charitable an act. So no more at present but remain

Your H'ble servant and well wisher
JOHN HOGE.

---

JOHN HOGE, PRISONER OF WAR, TO HIS FATHER.

COGNAC, March the 27th, 1757.

Honoured Father:

I take this opportunity of letting you know that I am well in health at present, thanks be to God for it, and I hope you enjoy the like blessing, although I have had my share of sickness, and but just coming to myself, it gives me a great deal of concern to think that I have the misfortune to be at so great a distance from you, but I hope when these few lines reach your hands it will revive your spirits, as I think you are doubtful whether I was dead or alive, and the way that I am now in. And knowing you always to be a tender and careful Father over me, a few lines with some relief from your hands would be a great comfort to me under my confinement, having but few clothes to put to my back, and if you would apply to Lord Thomas Fairfax he would put you in a way of sending it to me. Dear Father I should be glad you would send me an account how much you received of my wages, and what my team of horses was valued at, and whether you got my wagon that I left at Belhaven,[1] as I expect to

---

[1] Alexandria was frequently called Bell Haven. On February 20, 1755, General Braddock arrived at Alexandria, with two regiments from Ireland commanded by Col. Dunbar and Sir Peter Halket Braddock left the town on May 20th and marched by way of Winchester to the fatal battle-field at Fort Duquesne. John Hoge appears to have been attached to the expedition, in some capacity.

receive the remainder of my wages when I am released and arrive in England, of which I shall stand in need of to get my passage home, in which I hope to be a comfort to you after so long absence, and as it is troublesome times, get his Lordship to write to his friend, to get me a protection to keep me clear of a man of war. So no more at present but desires to be remembered to my brothers and sisters, uncles, and aunts and all enquiring friends, whilst I remain

Your ever loving and<br>dutiful son till death<br>JOHN HOGE.

P. S. It gives me a deal of satisfaction to let you know that there is a gentleman here that has been a great friend to me, and all my fellow prisoners, for which we have great reason to pray for his health and welfare, this gentleman's name is Anthony Le Measurer.

---

On August 30, 1757, William Fairfax died lamented for his many sterling qualities. Not only had he been president of the council of Virginia, but collector of the customs for the South Potomac.

### LITTLETON EYRE TO GEORGE W. FAIRFAX.

NORTHAMPTON, Sept'r 22, 1757.

Sir:

Since writing on the 20th inst, by our papers I see your Father is dead. His death occasions a vacancy in the Customs, probably you will endeavour for that place as I suppose it's better than your present one. If you will use your interest for your place on our Shore in my behalf so as to procure it for me or my son I will give you a hundred pounds. Pray let me know your sentiments on this affair and whether it will be in time to conclude on it at the October Court, and on what day, or if it is necessary to see you sooner I will meet you at any place you shall appoint

I am Sir, Your h'ble serv't

LITTLETON EYRE.

### LORD FAIRFAX TO GEO. W. FAIRFAX.

Dear George:

I have wrote a very pressing letter to my brother[1] to use his utmost endeavours to obtain

---

[1] Robert, the only brother and successor to the title.

for you the Collectorship of the South Potomack. I have acquainted him with the death of your father, and the great loss it must be to the whole family, which Mr. Martin[1] and myself heartily join in our sincerest condolence.

I considered as it would be so many days before the fleet sailed and there would be so many letters of solicitations that it would be impossible to keep it secret at home and therefore the best way was to own the whole truth.

I shall not fail writing on you from Prince W$^m$ Court on Wednesday the 23$^d$ of this instant, and Mr. Martin designs likewise to attend you, which is about the time Mr. Carlyle mentions. Pray make our compliments to Mrs. Fairfax and the rest of the good family on this melancholy occasion and you will oblige

Dear George Yours<br>FAIRFAX.

---

[1] Thomas Brian Martin was the nephew of the Lord, being a son of his sister Frances, and succeeded Geo. W. Fairfax, as the Lord's land agent.

In November, Mr. George W. Fairfax arrived in London to solicit from Lord Granville the office that had been held by his father.

---

### GEO. W. FAIRFAX TO LORD FAIRFAX.

LONDON, Dec'r 6th, 1757.

Sir:

In my last from Falmouth, I acquainted you of my arrival here on the 26th of last month, and the next day I waited on our worthy friend Mr. Athawes, who told me the vacant place was not then disposed of, and that the Commissioner of the Customs had recommended me to the Treasury, whereupon I went and had your kind letter delivered to the Duke of Newcastle, and then waited on Lord Granvile who kindly received me, and promised to do me any service in his power, and thus I rested till Mr. Fairfax came to town who waited on his Grace, and I hope has so far succeeded that I shall be appointed to that small place, which by some gentleman has been represented to be worth 5 or 6 hundred pounds per annum, and I believe has occasioned this delay.

The Parliament met the 1st, and unanimously agreed in a very loyal and dutiful address, in which they promise to aid the brave and victorious King of Prussia. The late second expedition against Rocford has unhappily miscarried, by I don't know whose neglect. But Sir John Mordaunt it seems is in custody, and to be tried by a court martial very soon, and it's whispered that Sir Edward Hawke will also be tried when he returns. Thus your Lordship may see how the Ministry have been imployed, and I heartily wish their orders may be better executed next campaign.

A Bill has passed already to prevent the exportation, and distillers using corn, etc., for one year occasioned by the great scarcity of it in the kingdom, whereby it is thought there will be sufficient to supply the people till next harvest, which if nothing particular happens will exceed any, as there never was so much put into the ground, as at the last sowing.

The execution of the Militia Law has occasioned great riots, and disturbances in many Counties, and a motion has been made in the House to bring in a Bill to amend it, which I

believe will be the principal business done before the holidays, which I shall spend in Kent, and then visit our relations and friends in Yorkshire. A convoy is appointed for our fleet in March, so that I hope I shall be so fortunate as to find you and friends well in April. I am my Lord
    Your Lordship's dutiful and
        most obliged humble servant
            Go. Wm. Fairfax.

---

GEORGE W. FAIRFAX TO HIS WIFE.

            London, Dec$^r$ 12$^{th}$ 1757.

Dear Sally:

I am sorry to say I have not yet succeeded and that it is uncertain whether I shall. But be it as it may, I find it was necessary to be here, and I should not have excused myself if I had not. Mr. Fairfax went down to Leeds Castle yesterday and left me to push my own way, and then to follow to spend my Christmas and to prepare for his imbarking with me in March. Therefore I beseech you'll employ old Tom, or get some person to put the garden in good order, and call upon Mr. Carlyle for his assistance in getting other necessary things done about the house in order to receive so fine a gentleman.[1] And I must further recommend, and desire that you'll endeavour to provide the best provision for his nice stomach, altho: I suppose he will spend chief of his time with his brother.

However to make his and other company more agreeable I shall endeavour to engage a butler to go over with me at least for one year.

My Dear, I have often wished for your company to enjoy the amusements of this Metropolis, for I can with truth say, they are not much so to me in my present situation and that I now and then go to a play only to kill time. But I please myself with my country visits imagining the time there will pass more agreeable. Permit me Sally to advise a steady and constant application to those things directed for your

---

[1] Robert, brother of Thomas Lord Fairfax, made the proposed visit. Washington, in one of his diaries, says: "Mr. Bryan Fairfax, Mr. Grayson, and Phil. Alexander, came home by sunrise. Hunted and catched a fox with these, Lord Fairfax, *his brother*, and Colonel Fairfax — all of whom, with Mr Fairfax and Mr Wilson of England, dined here."

welfare, which may afford me the greatest satisfaction upon my arrival.

Your affect. and loving husband
Go. Wm. Fairfax.

---

GEORGE LEE TO EDMUND ATHAWES, LONDON.

Sir:

If Col. Fairfax should be sailed for Virginia when this reaches you, be pleased to open the letter directed for him, negotiate the Bills of Exchange inclosed for his use and oblige

Yr most obed't h'ble serv't
George Lee.[1]

Virg'a Westmoreland, 2nd January, 1758.

---

[1] Lawrence Washington died at Mt. Vernon in 1752, and his widow, the sister of George Fairfax, married George Lee. Colonel George Washington, in a letter to Governor Dinwiddie on Aug. 14, 1756, says:

"As a general meeting of the persons concerned in the estate of my deceased brother is appointed to be held at Alexandria, about the middle of September, for making a final settlement of all his affairs, and as I am very deeply interested not only as an executor and heir of part of his estate, but also in a very important dispute subsisting between Colonel Lee who married the widow, and my brothers and self concerning a devise in the will * * * I hope your Honor will readily consent to my attending this meeting." George Lee was the uncle of Arthur and Richard Henry Lee, the revolutionary patriots.

LETTERS OF LORD FAIRFAX TO GEORGE W. FAIRFAX.

Dear George:

I received yours by Mr Andrews and am sorry to find you decline standing candidate for your County. I do propose being down at Prince William election, and so take either yours and London on my way up into Frederick. Our writ did not get to the sheriff's hands till this day by which means our election will be on Monday the twenty fourth of this month, and Hampshire will for the same reason be some days after it. I fear Coll. Washington will be very hard pushed.[1] My service attends Mrs Fairfax and all friends. Mr Martin is gone to Winchester, and I propose going thither to morrow. I remain

  Your humble servant & kinsman

      FAIRFAX.

July 5th 1758.

---

[1] He was hard pushed. There were three candidates, but he was successful. Sparks says the election cost Washington £39 6s., and among the items of the bill were a hogshead and a barrel of punch, thirty-five gallons of wine, forty-three gallons of strong beer, cider, and dinner for his friends.

Dear George:

Mr. Neil[1] has been with me and complains that Joseph Carter takes in all the water, which very much hurts his plantation. He desires if he have thirty or forty acres which I really think is very reasonable. He likewise desires his brother's and his deed may be made separate.

I should be likewise glad if some Golden Pipen, Nonparel, Aromatick and Medlar Apple grafts by him, which he will take care to convey to me. My service attends Mrs. Fairfax and all friends. I remain Yours

FAIRFAX.

Sept'r 10th 1758.

Dear George:

Mr. Stephens in his way to the office called here and I take the opportunity of sending by him a letter left here for you, as also Mr

---

[1] Mr. Neill was an Irish Quaker settled on the Opequan, about five miles from Winchester, and was sheriff of Frederick county.

A descendant of his, Lt. Lewis Neill, a graduate of West Point, distinguished himself in the Mexican war, and died at Fort Croghan, Texas.

Lemons plot. When you see Mr Carlyle pray desire him to set aside a hogshead of rum and barrel of sugar which I shall soon send my wagon for. I believe I shall be down in your parts before you set out for Williamsburgh. Mr Baylis has very much disappointed us, in not sending up a plan of Winchester, which has prevented my sending down a petition for the addition to Winchester, which as Mr Wood is doing may occasion some confusion. Hollingsworth[1] is likewise desirous of doing the same thing, as also Mr Cocken. My service attends the families at Belvoir and Alexandria. I remain

    Your humble servant and kinsman

                FAIRFAX.

---

The following letter was taken from the Fairfax manuscripts in 1860, and given by a

---

[1] Fothergill, the Quaker preacher, and brother of the celebrated physician, in 1736 visited "Abraham Hollingsworth, a Friend near Opeckon."

Valentine Hollingsworth, a Friend, settled in New Castle county, Del., about 1682. His son Henry moved to Elkton, Md. and he had a number of sons who became heads of families in Virginia, Maryland, Delaware and Pennsylvania.

gentleman, who had married the granddaughter of Bryan, Lord Fairfax, to the late Hon. Edward Everett.[1]

It was addressed to Miss Mary Cary by Col. George Washington, while in camp near the Pennsylvania line, thirty miles from Fort Cumberland, awaiting the slow movements of General Forbes.

He had been sincerely attached to her, and always maintained friendly relations, but was prevented from marrying her by the unwillingness of her father. Bishop Meade, in his *History of Old Churches in Virginia* prints a document of the Ambler family, an extract from which throws some light on this early love of Washington. It says:

"The eldest sister of Miss Mary Cary had married George William Fairfax, at whose house she was on a visit, when she captivated a young man who paid her his addresses. His affection, however, was not returned, and the offer of his hand was rejected by Miss Cary.

---

[1] Mr. Everett incorporated it in his article on Washington in the *New American Cyclopedia* and supposed it was addressed to the widow, Martha Custis.

This young man was afterward known to the world as General George Washington, the first President of the United States of America.

"Young Washington asked permission of old Mr. Cary to address his daughter before he ventured to speak to herself. The reply of the old gentleman was, 'If that is your business here, Sir, I wish you to leave the house, for my daughter has been accustomed to ride in her own coach.'

"It has subsequently been said that this answer of Mr. Cary to the stripling Washington, produced the independence of the United States, and laid the foundation of the future fame of the first of braves and the best of men — our immortal Washington; as it was more than probable that, had he obtained possession of the large fortune which it was known Miss Cary would carry to the altar with her, he would have passed the remainder of his life in inglorious ease.

"It was an anecdote of the day that this lady, many years after she had been the wife of Edward Ambler, happened to be in Williamsburg when General Washington passed through that city at the head of the American army, crowned with never fading laurels, and adored by his countrymen. Having distinguished her among the crowd, his sword waved toward her a military salute, whereupon she is said to have fainted. But this wants confirmation, for her whole life tended to show that she never for a moment regretted the choice she had made. It may be added as a curious fact that the lady General Washington afterward married resembled Miss Cary as much as one twin-sister ever did another."

COL. GEO. WASHINGTON TO MISS MARY CARY.

CAMP AT RAYS TOWN, 25th Sept'r, 1758.

Dear Madam:

Do we still misunderstand the true meaning of each other's Letters? I think it must appear so, tho' I would feign hope the contrary as I cannot speak plainer without —— but I'll say no more and leave you to guess the rest.

I am now furnished with News of a very interesting nature, I know it will affect you, but as you must hear it from others I will state it myself. The 12th past, then Major Grant with a chosen Detachment of 800 men march'd from our advanced post at Loyal Hanna against Fort Du-quesne.

On the night of the 13th he arrivd at that place or rather upon a Hill near to it; from whence went a party and viewd the Works, made what observations they could, and burnt a Logd house not far from the Walls. Egg'd on rather than satisfied by this success, Major Grant must needs insult the Enemy next morning by beating the Reveille in different places in view, this caus'd a great body of men to Sallie from the Fort, and an obstinate engagement to ensue, which was maintained on our Side with the utmost efforts that bravery could yield, till being overpower'd and quite surrounded they were obliged to Retreat with the loss of 22 officers killed, and 278 men besides wounded.

This is a heavy blow to our Affairs here, and a sad stroke upon my Regiment, that has lost out of 8 officers, and 168 that was in the Action, 6 of the former killd, and a 7th wounded. Among the Slain was our dear Major Lewis;

this Gentleman as the other officers also did, bravely fought while they had life, tho' wounded in different places. Your old acquaintance Capt'n Bullet, who is the only officer of mine that came of untouched has acquired immortal honour in this engagement by his gallant behaviour, and long continuance in the field of Action. It might be thought vanity in me to praise the behaviour of my own People were I to deviate from the report of common Fame,— but when you consider the loss they have sustaind, and learn that every mouth resounds their praises, you will believe me Impartial.

What was the great end proposed by this attempt or what will be the want of its failure, I cant take upon me to determine; it appears however (from the best Accts) that the Enemy lost more men then we did in the engagement. Thus it is the Lives of the brave are often disposed of— but who is there that does not rather Envy than regret a Death that gives birth to Honour and Glorious memory.

I am extremely glad to find that Mr Fairfax[1]

---

[1] Wm. Henry Fairfax, brother of Geo. W. and Bryan Fairfax, was an ensign of the 28th British regulars. The

has escap'd the Dangers of the Siege at Louisbourg. Already have we experienced greater Losses than our Army sustaind at that place, and have gain'd not one obvious Advantage. So miserably has this Expedition been managd that I expect after a month's further Tryal, and the loss of many more men by the Sword, Cold and perhaps Famine, we shall give the expedition over as perhaps impracticable this season, and retire to the inhabitants, condemnd by the World and derided by our Friends.

I shoud think our time more agreeable spent believe me, in playing a part in Cato, with the company you mention, and myself doubly happy in being the Juba to such a Marcia as you must make.[1]

Your agreeable Letter containd these words "My Sisters and Nancy Gist who neither of them expect to be here soon after our return

---

next year he was fatally wounded at the storming of Quebec. Archdeacon Burnaby says that General Wolfe saw him as the army landed, seated near the bank of the river, and that touching him on the shoulder, said: " *Young man, when we come to action remember your name.*"

[1] Addison's tragedy of Cato must have been full of interest to the young military officer in love with a fair maiden,

from Town, desire you to accept their best complimts &c."

Pray are these Ladies upon a Matrimonial

---

and yet debarred from being her husband, because her father looked upon him, as without fortune, and without fame.

Many passages in the play are exceedingly apposite to one in his situation, but only a few can be given:

Act I, Scene 5th.

*Juba.* O Marcia, let me hope thy kind concerns
And gentle wishes follow me to battle.

*Marcia.* My prayers and wishes always shall attend
The friends of Rome, the glorious cause of virtue,
And men approv'd of the gods and Cato.

*Juba.* Thou virtuous maid: I'll hasten to my troops
\* \* \* \* \* \* \*
And in the shock of charging hosts, remember
What glorious deeds, should grace the man, who hopes
For Marcia's love.

Act IV, Scene 1st.

*Marcia.* Juba to all the bravery of a hero,
Adds softest love, and more than female sweetness;
Juba might make the proudest of our sex,
Any of woman kind, but Marcia happy.

*Lucia.* And why not Marcia? \* \* \*

*Marcia.* While *Cato lives, his daughter has no right*
*To love or hate but as his choice directs.*

Act IV, Scene 3d.

*Marcia.* Why do I think on what he was! He's dead!
He's dead, and never knew how much I loved him.
\* \* \* \* \* \* \* \*

Scheme? Is Miss Fairfax[1] to be transformed into that charming Domestick — a Martin, and Miss Cary[2] to a Fa-re. What does Miss Gist turn to — A Cocke[3] that cant be, we have him here.

One thing more and then have done. You ask if I am not tird at the length of your letter? No Madam I am not, nor never can be while the Lines are an Inch assunder to bring you in haste to the end of the Paper, you may be tird of mine by this. Adieu dear Madam, you will possibly hear something of me, or from me before we

---

*Juba.*   Where am I? do I live! or am indeed
        What Marcia thinks! all is Elysium around me.
*Marcia.* Ye dear remains of the most loved of men!
        Nor modesty, nor virtue here forbid
        A last embrace while thus
*Juba.*   See Marcia! See!
        The happy Juba lives, he lives to catch
        That dear embrace, and to return it too
        With mutual warmth and eagerness of love."

[1] Hannah Fairfax, sister of Wm. Henry and Bryan, afterwards married Warner Washington, and not as suggested Mr. Martin, the nephew of Thomas, sixth Lord Fairfax.

[2] Elizabeth, the sister of Mary Cary, married soon after this letter was written, Bryan, subsequently the eighth Lord Fairfax.

[3] Captain Cocke was then an officer of one of the Virginia companies.

shall meet. I must beg the favour of you to make my compliments to Col° Cary and the Ladies with you, and believe me that I am most unalterably

Y'r most Obedt. and Oblig'd
G° WASHINGTON.

Tradition relates that in the year 1758, while Washington was traveling to Williamsburg, after crossing the Pumunkey river ferry, he was invited by a gentleman of New Kent county to tarry with him during the night, and was then introduced to the prepossessing and dignified young widow, Martha Custis.[1]

Repelled by the father of her whom he had loved from early youth, and yet longing for one in whom he could confide, the widow made a deep impression upon him, and after a brief acquaintance he was accepted as her future husband.

The prediction made in his letter to Miss Cary, "*You will hear something of me, or from me,*" was fulfilled. On the 25th of November

---

[1] Custis's *Recollections of Washington*, New York, 1859.

the heroic young officer planted the British flag on the ruins of Fort Duquesne, which the French had evacuated and burned at his approach. Returning to Virginia he hastened to the house of burgesses of which he had been elected a member while with the army, and early in January, 1759, he was married at the White House, to Mrs. Martha Custis by the Rev. David Mossom of St. Peter's parish, New Kent county.

He made the widow's house his home during his attendance upon the legislature. The first month of married life was hardly over, when, says Bancroft, "in the House of Burgesses, the Speaker obeying the resolve of the House, publicly gave him the thanks of Virginia for his services to his country; and when the young man, taken by surprise, hesitated for words, as he rose to reply, 'Sit down,' rejoined the speaker, 'your modesty is equal to your valor, and that surpasses the power of any language I possess.'"

LORD FAIRFAX TO GEO. W. FAIRFAX.

Feb'y 16th 1759.

Dear George:

Yours I this evening received and shall be very sorry if Mr. Mason should be able to carry a point so prejudicial to the three counties of Fairfax, Loudon, and Prince W$^m$. If the Lees[1] and Custis should join in the affair, I doubt they with the assistance of James River

---

[1] Col. Philip Lee was one of the descendants of Richard Lee, an early settler in Virginia, who is spoken of in the records of England (1654) as "Colonel Lee faithful and useful to the interest of the Commonwealth," and thus in sympathy with Digges, Bennett and others who upheld parliament.

His son Richard was a prominent man in the colony and a fine scholar. On his tombstone in Westmoreland county is a Latin inscription, to this effect:

"Here lieth the body of Richard Lee, Esq., born in Virginia, son of Richard Lee, Gentleman, descended of an old family of Merton-Regis in Shropshire.

"While he exercised the office of a magistrate, he was a zealous promoter of the public good.

"He was well versed in Greek and Latin literature, and other branches of polite learning.

"To God, whom he always adored with the greatest reverence, he tranquilly resigned his soul on the twelfth day of March 1714 in the 68th year of his age."

He left five sons:

1. Richard, who became a London merchant and was the

will carry it in the House of Assembly. I will therefore write to Col's Philip Lee, and Col. Tayloe and try what we can do in the Upper House. I have just received an angry letter

---

father of George Lee, who married the widow of Lawrence Washington.

2. Philip moved to Maryland.
3. Francis.
4. Thomas.
5. Henry.

Thomas, the fourth son, by industry and intelligence became wealthy. He married a Miss Hannah Ludwell, and had six sons.

1. Philip, referred to in the above letter, who married Miss Steptoe. His eldest daughter became the wife of General Lee, the Light Horse Harry of the revolution, who was the father of Gen. Robert Lee, now president of Washington College, Va.

2. Thomas, who married a Miss Aylett.

3. Richard Henry Lee, born in 1732, educated in England, member of the first Continental congress, president of congress of 1784, one of the first senators of Virginia under the constitution. Died 1794.

4. Francis Lightfoot, born in 1734, married Rebecca, daughter of John Tayloe, member of Continental congress and signer of the Declaration of Independence. Died 1797.

5. William, sheriff of the city of London, and U. S. commissioner at Berlin and Vienna.

6. Arthur, born in 1740, first studied medicine at Edinburgh, then law in London. Member of Continental congress from 1781 to 1784. Died 1792.

from Charles Carter[1] wherein he desires me to send him an account by Col. Martin, what his arrears of quit rent amount to, which is not in my power to do. I hope shortly to see you. My service attends Mrs. Fairfax.

I remain Yours
FAIRFAX.

Ten at night.

EDWARD ATHAWES TO GEO. W. FAIRFAX.

LONDON, 24 Nov'r 1759.

Dear Sir:

I have just now rec'd the inclosed letter for you from the Rev. Mr. Mosley of York. He tells me it is of the utmost importance, as it informs you of the dying condition of your Uncle. I send it by the post to Portsmouth, in expectation of getting it on board of a ship now there, and bound to Virginia, under cover to Richard Ambler Esq. with a request to for-

---

[1] The ancestor of the Carter family first settled in Upper Norfolk or Nansemond county, and was its burgess in 1649. In 1654 he appears as burgess from Lancaster county.

Robert, his descendant, was agent of the Fairfax estates,

ward it immediately to you. I have not heard any thing from Leeds Castle for a great while, nor do I see a line from you by any of our Virginia fleet, now arrived at Portsmouth with the Lynn, Man of War.

My whole family are in the greatest anxiety on account of our dear friend, your brother Mr. W<sup>m</sup> Hen<sup>y</sup> Fairfax who the Gazette informed us long since was wounded at the battle of Quebeck.[1] God grant he may be well. We all esteem and love him, so do all who know him. My respects of duty wait on L'd Fairfax, to his and your whole family. I am

    Your affectionate & obliged
        humble servant
            EDWD. ATHAWES.

---

but giving dissatisfaction was superseded by William Fairfax, the ancestor of the Virginia Fairfaxes. Robert was called King Carter. Charles was a grandson of Robert.

[1] The wound was fatal.

GEO. W. FAIRFAX TO ROBERT CARTER NICHOLAS.

April 1761.

Dear Sir:

I shall proceed to tell you that during my absence and indisposition, there were some very sudden changes in our Ministry, among which was Lord Halifax who I suppose had a mind to make the most of his place at the Board of Trade.

Without considering he appointed an under clerk and Mr Nelson [1] Naval officers in the room of our friend Colonel Cary [2] and poor old Church-

---

[1] Mr. Nelson was the son of Thomas Nelson who came to Virginia in 1705, and a merchant at Yorktown, often called Scotch Tom, because he came from Penriff on the borders of Scotland.

[2] Colonel Wilson Miles Cary was the descendant of an early Virginia settler. Miles, son of John Cary of Bristol, England, arrived in the colony in 1640, and settled in Warwick county. He died in 1667, leaving four sons, two of whom, Thomas and Miles appear to have been Quakers.

Story, the classical and logical Quaker preacher, in his journal under date of 19th of 12 month, 1699, says "Went to Thomas Carey's who had been lately convinced. His wife had been also. His brother Miles and wife coming hither to see us, were made partakers of the same visitation."

Six years later, Story writes: " made a visit to Miles Carey

ill who of the two I pity, for the other thank God has an independent fortune and can live very well without.

But yet it is amazing that old officers who have discharged their duty so long without the least complaint, should be turned out. * * *

Your affect and very humble serv't

G. W. FAIRFAX.

---

GEO. W. FAIRFAX TO LORD FAIRFAX.

BELVOIR, May 1, 1760.

My Lord:

Upon account of your Lordship's affairs, I had concluded to stay till I had settled them to my satisfaction, but I have just rec'd another letter from my friend in Yorkshire, requiring my

---

Secretary of the County, who being absent his wife a Friend prevailed with us to stay to supper."

Col. Wilson Miles Cary had been collector of the lower district of James river for thirty-four years, and was a gentleman of culture and wealth.

His daughter Sarah married Geo. Wm. Fairfax; his daughter Elizabeth married Bryan, brother of George, afterwards eighth Lord Fairfax; and Anna became the wife of the distinguished Robert Carter Nicholas to whom the above letter was written, and Mary, the early love of Washington, married Edward Ambler.

immediate presence to put a stop to the foreclosing of the mortgage on the Redness estate, which obliges me to alter my resolution and to prepare for embarking in the first good ship from this River, so shall be glad to know whether you have thought of any person to keep the Office, and how the books are to be disposed of, for I am afraid I cant accomplish my trip under twelve or eighteen months, in which time the business might suffer. Mr Carlyle has informed me that you signified a desire of removing down, which I wish could be convenient and then the same hand now in the office, and under your Eye and direction could continue the business, but if that be not agreeable, and you have no person in view I will endeavour to leave things in the best situation I can, and I am certain Mr Dent is so well qualified now, that he can do and keep all the ordinary business, and if you have a mind the several receivers may be directed to make their returns of money to you, or any person you may please to direct. The Rev Mr Green[1] has

---

[1] Rev. Charles Green was from Ireland, and minister of old Pohick church in Truro parish, Fairfax county, from 1738

kindly offered you or me any service in his power, and I think when there is any intricate affair, I dont know of any that I would sooner accept, for he has been formerly well acquainted with the office business, and is able to examine any plot that can be brought before him. Or I dare say Col: Washington could inspect into these affairs during my absence. But these methods I only mention in case you have not fixed upon any one for these purposes, for I am far from desiring the continuance of the business, but would willingly do all in my power to increase your revenue. * * * I am getting things ready to repair the house, and if your Lordship is inclined I will endeavour to make it as agreeable as possible, and truly say you shall be heartily welcome. I am with all due regard

 Your Lordships most obliged and
    very humble servant
      Go. Wm. Fairfax.

---

until his death in 1765. In his will he recommends that his wife shall return to Ireland. He was intimately associated with his parishioners George Mason, George Washington and George William Fairfax, all of whom were vestrymen in 1765. At times he practised medicine.

BELVOIR, May 27, 1760.

My Lord:

Since your Lordships departure Sally tells me that Col Martin said you would not object to reside here in our absence, and as we did not talk on the subject I shall be very glad if you'll leave a line with Mr Carlyle to let me know if you'll choose any of the house servants should remain here.

Col Martin it seems, told Mrs Fairfax that your Lordship would choose to bring down your own furniture, bed, table and chairs, except that they are troublesome to remove. The house, and every thing in it, is at your service, and all or any part of the negroes you think proper. I desire no rent for the house and plantation, as it will be an advantage to have them inhabited, and if your Lordship would choose any of the negroes should remain please fix your own terms. * * * * * There are many matters relative to your office, I should be glad to talk about, which I flatter myself will tend to your interest, and I hope you'll order your affairs at Greenway Court, so that you'll spend some days when you come down next, when I hope to have more leisure and less company

    Your L'dships humb servt
       G. W. F.

My Lord:

I was much concerned upon my arrival here to find that your Lordship had left Williamsburg.

As I intended doing myself the honor of waiting on you the next day to receive any commands you might have for England, and again more particularly obtaining your permission of absence for a few years about some private affairs of great consequence to myself and family.

If your Lordship thinks your written leave is necessary I shall be greatly obliged to your Excellency, if you'll favour me with a line directed to the care of Mr Sam¹ Athawes merch't in London

  Your Lordships most obed't and
    most obliged h'ble serv't
      G°. W<small>M</small>. F<small>AIRFAX</small>.

### JOSIAH CLAPHAM[1] TO GEO. W. FAIRFAX.

Sir:

When you arrive at the City of York, please be kind enough to write my wife a line advising where she may meet with you there, and I make no doubt she will immediately wait on you I having instructed her so to do. Then please direct her to whom, and in what manner she must apply for her and my boy's passage into Virginia, and in doing this you will add to your favours, the greatest obligation imaginable and forever bind to your services Hon'd Sir

Your most gratefull and most obed't
h'ble servant to command
Jo: Clapham.

N. B. She lives in Wakefield.

---

[1] The Claphams were associated with the Fairfaxes for several generations. A Mr. Clapham was private chaplain of Henry, fourth Lord Fairfax in 1684.

Dorothy Fairfax, sister of William Fairfax, the founder of Belvoir, Va., was the wife of a Mr. H. Clapham who resided at Hull, England.

Josiah Clapham of Virginia was one of the trustees named in the act incorporating the town of Leesburg, and member of the convention of 1775.

### GEO. W. FAIRFAX TO GEORGE WASHINGTON.

LONDON, April 15th 1761.

Dear Sir:

I came to town about some business of Col. Cary's, and could by no means omit so good an opportunity as by the Convoy to enquire after your, and good Mrs Washington's welfare, and to let you know that it was with difficulty I got here, and that poor Mrs Fairfax and I have alternately been confined to our chambers since we have been in England, but I hope as the warm weather approaches we shall both get better. It is impossible for me to fix the time for my return, but I shall do every thing in my power to bring it within the time first limited. * * * * The chief news and talk of the Metropolis is of immediate peace, and the King's marriage[1] with the young Princess of Brunswick

---

[1] Massey, speaking of the marriage of George III, says: "High-breeding and personal merit was no qualification for the consort of a British Sovereign. Royal blood is the one thing needful and that was provided for in the person of a Princess of one of those diminutive Sovereignties, which bring ridicule on the royal dignity.

"Homely in person, of narrow and uncultivated understanding was Charlotte of Mecklenburg Strelitz * * *

"That such a woman should have been productive of

not quite fifteen years of age, but I believe neither certain tho' the stocks rise every day, and it is said the expedition Fleet is arrived and landed men at Bellisle in the Bay, but Sir Edward Hawke who is just returned from thence, says he left nothing but fishing vessels, the French having broken up and burnt all the ships that they could not get out to sea, and have removed all their valuables to the interiour parts. The changes and other particulars I shall refer you to the magazine herewith inclosed, and I wish I could say they were satisfactory to the people * * *

Mrs Fairfax and I, thank God are upon the recovery and hope Buxton Wells strongly recommended will set us both quite right, and enable us to return within the time limited, but in the meantime should be glad to know your and Mr Green's determination about leaving that part of the world,[1] for I assure you 'tis our

---

domestic happiness could hardly have been expected but nevertheless it was attended with that good fortune."

[1] George Washington in a letter to Richard Washington of London, dated August 10, 1760, alludes to an invitation to visit England in these words:

" My indulging myself in a trip to England depends upon

greatest inducement, and will turn the scale very much whether we come back or not. Pray make my compliments to Mrs Green, Miss Bolan, and all our worthy neighbours, and believe me with greatest esteem Dear Sir

Your affect. and very humb. servt

Go. Wm. Fairfax.

June 5th 1761.

Mrs Fairfax:

To H. Ambler Dr.

|  |  | £. | s. | d. |
|---|---|---|---|---|
| | For making blew and white silck night gown | 0. | 3. | 0 |
| | body lining to do | 0. | 1. | 0 |
| | pd for 9 yds pea green rib. | 0. | 1. | 6 |
| | for 4 yds ½ of broad | 0. | 1. | 6 |
| | for mending crape gown | 0. | 1. | 0 |
| | for trimming black short apron | 0. | 1. | 0 |
| | pd for silck for trimming do | 0. | 2. | 6 |
| Aug. 22nd | for making black silck negligee and coat | 0. | 7. | 0 |
| | for making trimmings and trimming do | 0. | 8. | 0 |
| | for body and sleeves linings | 0. | 1. | 6 |
| | for ferritt buttons, looping and | 0. | 1. | 9 |
| | pd for 6 dozen 8 yds of black rib | 0. | 16. | 3· |
| | pd for 10 yds of rich black silck | 7. | 12. | 0 |
| | 1 walking Grey Lustring negligee | 0. | 2. | 0 |
| | | £10. | 0. | 0 |

Received March the 17th the above contents and all demands.

Hannah Ambler.

---

so many contingencies which in all probability may never occur, that I dare not even think of such gratification."

GEO. W. FAIRFAX TO GEORGE WASHINGTON.

October 30th 1761.

Dear Sir:

Your favour of the 2nd of December, 6th of March, 3d of April, 27th of July and first of August came very safe to hand. In that of July, I am sorry to find that you were in such a bad state of health,[1] and that neither Mr Green's nor Mr Hamilton's prescriptions had the desired effect. The latter's it seems you had but just begun and consequently could not expect an immediate cure, but I hope long before this you are perfectly restored. If not probably change of air might be of service, and if you had any particular business, or even fancy to see England, we shall be extremely glad to see you at York, or at our little retreat not many miles from it.

But I hope a bad state of health will not oblige you to cross the horrible Ocean, tho' if better advice should be really necessary the

---

[1] George Washington, in a letter to Richard Washington of London, alludes to his sickness in 1761, and says: "I once thought the grim King would certainly master my utmost efforts." — *Sparks's Washington*, vol. II, p. 336.

sooner it is taken the better, and not delay it so long as our deceased friend. I am very sorry my mare Moggy did not prove with foal, and that I should have neglected to desire that you would put her to whatever horse you thought proper. It may possibly be occasioned from her travelling so great a distance after, and suppose you were to try your own horse Gift in the spring. It will be the least trouble and certainly will remove the suspicion. I am informed by many hands, tho' not from the performers, that an Office is really building at Greenway Court,[1] and that his Lordship and family removes this very month. It gives me the most concern to find what an influence, Martin has, as I fear he will not stop at that, but will daily lessen the esteem the people have for the good old Gent$^n$. I offer my compliments to Mrs Washington and am very sincerely dear Sir,

  Your most ob't humble serv't
    Go. Wm. Fairfax.

---

[1] Under the influence of his nephew, Col. T. B. Martin, Thomas Lord Fairfax moved the land office from Belvoir to Greenway Court, twelve miles southeast of Winchester.

I have been endeavouring ever since I have been in England to get a gardener or two, but without success.

---

GEO. W. FAIRFAX TO MR. FAIRFAX OF KENT IN 1716.

Dear Sir:

By the last post I had a line from our friend Mr Athawes advising that the Rev Mr Thos. Dawson [1] Commissary, died since I left Virginia, whereby there is a vacant seat in the Council, and shall take it as a favour if you would apply to Lords Halifax and Granville to nominate and appoint either Mr Martin or Colonel Presly Thornton [2] to succeed him.

As Mr Thornton is a stranger I must acquaint you that he is a gentleman of property in the Northern Neck, and I dare say will be a friend

---

[1] Rev. Thomas Dawson succeeded his brother, Rev. William, as commissary of the bishop of London. Bishop Meade says that in his latter years he became addicted to drink.

[2] Col. Presley Thornton was one of the most influential men of the Northern Neck, and in 1777 was a member of Washington's military family.

His son Presley was a British army officer at the time of the revolution, but would not fight against his country.

to the Proprietor thereof which is much wanting at that board. * * * I have long observed that the lower members disregard and look upon the Northern Neck as a separate interest, tho' under the same laws. Whenever you are in a prospect of succeeding, if you'll let me know I will advance the money usually paid for the warrant.

---

TO THE BISHOP OF LONDON.

YORK, Oct. 1761.

My Lord:

Mr Leonard Watson having a very strong desire for entering into Holy Orders, and to remove to the Colony of Virginia has applied to me as an inhabitant thereof for a recommendation upon which I have made great inquiry and with pleasure find that he bears a general good character and I hope your Lordship will find him qualified for ordination. The vestry of each parish upon a vacancy are empowered by law to elect their minister within a year, but if they should fail to do so, in that time, then the Governor or Commander in chief may appoint, so that Gentlemen that come over to be ordained seldom, or indeed ever apply for a title, or can have the assurance of a particular parish, this I took the liberty to mention to your Lordship, as I understand it is required of those that reside in England.

I am my Lord
Your Lordship's most obedient humble serv't
G. W. FAIRFAX of Virginia.

GEO. W. FAIRFAX TO HON. MR. FAIRFAX OF ENGLAND.
ASKAM NEAR YORK, Sept'r 8, 1762.

Dear Sir:

As it was not convenient for you, Mr and Miss Martin to come to our last years races, I was in hopes it would have suited you this, and wrote to you about a month before they happened by Mr Carcart who had business at Rochester, to beg the favour of your company, and till they were over, I must own I pleased myself with the expectation. Upon my friend Mr Croft's return from London, I had the pleasure of hearing of you, and since by Mr Athawes, and the former said you was surprized at not seeing me in town, a place, good Sir, I avoid as much as possible from the expensiveness of it, but if you had any particular reason for desiring it, I would cheerfully attend you there or wherever you think proper. Mr Croft did inform my friend Mosley that you said it was expedient for me to return to America. But upon what account I know not for I dare say that you must be acquainted that Mr M————[1] has carried his long laboured point of getting the management of the Office into his own hands, and removing it with them to Frederick, so that unless it's my own private affairs that require my presence I know of no other, for I have been hitherto, and can be indulged by the Commissioner of Customs, till I completed the business that called me over. Indeed upon the confirmation of this point being carried, I was more concerned upon my good Lord's account than upon my own, for I thank my stars, I can stand the utmost screwing, and have enough for me and my wife to live retired upon.

Your ever obliged humble serv't<br>
G° W<small>M</small>. F<small>AIRFAX</small>.

---

[1] Thos. B. Martin, nephew of Lord Fairfax.

GEO. W. FAIRFAX TO RICHARD WASHINGTON.

Oct. 7, 1762.

Dear Sir:

Upon my return the other day I found your favour of the 23ᵈ of September, covering some musick for my sister, who returns her thanks for your remembrance of her. I was surprised to find our friends had left Yorkshire, and more so that they had not discovered who it was that disconcerted their scheme. I left this place the 5ᵗʰ ult, and only arrived two or three days ago. In my tour I had the satisfaction of seeing Scotland, my friends at Carlisle, Whitehaven, and along the coast to Liverpool, and now am determined to fix to business, and get every thing settled if possible, a month before my departure to London, and you'll assist me greatly, if you will apply for what may remain of my salary at the Custom House. By some of the last ships from Virginia I had a line from Mr Cary, and Col W————[1] they give a most terrible account of the crops there, and the horrid prospect the people have before

---

[1] Colonel Washington.

them. Corn what used to be 5 and 6 shillings a barrel is now thirty five shillings.

Your namesake[1] says he is pretty well recovered, and does not now mention any word of his coming over. Not a line from Mr Carlyle, but expect that satisfaction by the fleet. The Ladies join in their compliments.

Your affect. humble serv't<br>G°. W<small>M</small>. F<small>AIRFAX</small>.

---

### GEO. W. FAIRFAX TO HON. ROBERT[2] FAIRFAX OF ENGLAND.

A<small>SKAM NEAR</small> Y<small>ORK</small>, Nov'r 16, 1762.

Dear Sir:

Upon my return from a tour in the North, I received a line from Mr Washington, which gave me vast pleasure as it acquainted me of your having been in town, and in good health for I was really unhappy by not hearing from you for so long a time.

---

[1] Washington.

[2] Robert, brother of Thomas, sixth Lord Fairfax, and successor to the title.

Mr W—— also said you signified an intention of going to Virginia in the Spring if there was peace by that time, & as it now seems in great forwardness I have some thoughts of embarking there with my family, and shall be extremely glad of such good company, and shall do every thing in my power to make our cottage in that wooded world, as tolerable to you as possible. Do, my good Sir, think seriously of this and resolve to go. I really think it would be much to your interest to see once what must shortly be your property, for sorry I am to inform you that by letters from many of my friends, I find, that my good Lord is much broken and declines fast,[1] and it's also hinted to me that my Lord is made very unhappy, which in some measure accounts for his desire of returning to England. We propose being in town two or three months before we imbark, and shall hope to have the good fortune of meeting with you there. In the meantime it will give me great pleasure to have a line from

---

[1] Thomas, sixth Lord Fairfax, survived twenty years and died at Greenway Court, 1782.

you. My wife and sister present their compliments and I am with great esteem dear Sir

Yours &c.
G° W<small>M</small>. F<small>AIRFAX</small>.

---

LORD ROBERT FAIRFAX TO GEO. W. FAIRFAX.
G<small>REENWAY</small> C<small>OURT</small>, 19th Oct. 1768.

Dear Sir:

I have mentioned the affair we talked of to my brother, he seems to make some doubts about it, as he says that he has promised the tenants to grant them leases; however he says he will consider of it. * * * * My brother is determined to make you a visit as soon as your return to Belvoir, and hopes you will return as soon as you can, that the hunting season may not be too far advanced. He desires that you will let us know when you will be at home, that he may come to you as soon as possible. I need not tell you that I've no news for I have seen nothing since I have been here but *Buckskins*.[1] I am at all times and places

Your affectionate kinsman
R. F<small>AIRFAX</small>.

---

[1] Buckskins, a term applied to frontiersmen.

GEO. W. FAIRFAX TO CAPT. THOMAS EDEN.

BELVOIR, May 10, 1773.

Sir:

I am told by Col. Washington, that his Excellency, Governor Eden,[1] informed him it would be agreeable to you to take passengers to London, which occasions my taking the liberty to address you and to beg to be informed as nearly as possible of the time when you expect to sail, where the ship will lay, and what are your terms for cabin, and steerage passengers. My wife, two servants and myself at the most, with our baggage is all I propose carrying. * * * I am Sir

Your most ob't humb. servt

G° W<small>M</small> F<small>AIRFAX</small>.

---

[1] Governor Eden of Maryland married Caroline, daughter of Charles, fifth Lord Baltimore, and was governor from 1769 until 1776, when the populace obliged him to leave the country.

After the war he returned and soon died, and was buried under the pulpit of an Episcopal church on the north side of the Severn, two or three miles from Annapolis.

RICHARD CORBIN TO GEO. W. FAIRFAX.

LANEVILLE, 16th Aug'st, 1773.

Dear Sir:

I could not let Captain Punderson leave this place, without acknowledging the receipt of your kind letter from York, which in very few words contained every thing the warmest friendship could dictate. Mrs Fairfax's kind assurance makes my wife quite easy and happy, and that Frank is so I make no doubt. My wife indeed my whole family join with me in their best wishes for you and Mrs Fairfax. To hear of your safe arrival in England will give joy to your friends, to none more than this family and Dear Sir

Your most humb. and ob't serv't

R'D CORBIN.[1]

---

[1] Henry, the ancestor of the Corbins, settled in King and Queen county about 1650. His son, Gawin, became president of the council of Virginia, and married a daughter of William Bassett, and had four daughters and three sons, one of whom, Richard, was the writer of the above letter. In 1754, Washington wrote to Mr. Corbin, stating that he would be pleased to receive a commission as lieutenant colonel. Through Mr. Corbin's influence as a member of the Virginia council, it was obtained and transmitted with the following laconic note:

FRANCIS WILLIS, AGENT OF GEO. W. FAIRFAX.

LEESBURG, September 15th 1773.

Hon'ble Sir:

I impatiently waited the return of Miles expecting to have been informed of your resolutions respecting the renting of your house. * * You have not even hinted to me what you expect per year, what time or number of years to let it for, nor have you desired it to be rented from year to year. I think it would be better to rent it on very low terms, than to suffer it to be uninhabited. Upon the receipt of your letter by Miles, I waited on Col. G. Washington, and after a day or two's consideration we resolved to decline renting the house or selling the furniture until we could be directed by you. * *

Your very obedient servant
FRANCIS WILLIS Jun'r.

---

Dear George:

I inclose you your commission. God prosper you with it.
Your friend,
RICHARD CORBIN.

He lived at Laneville on the Mattapony, in King and Queen county, and his wife was a daughter of Colonel John Tayloe.

His son Frank was sent to England with Hon. G. W. Fairfax, to be educated.

ROBERT CARTER NICHOLAS TO GEO. W. FAIRFAX.

VIRG'A, 16th Oct[r], 1773.

My dear Sir:

The interest I hold in your own and my sister Fairfax's welfare makes me exceedingly anxious to hear of your happy arrival in England, and safe recovery from the small pox. I shall be sadly disappointed if the first ship from London, does not bring us this agreeable news. * * * We must therefore have patience, and a great deal I fear will be necessary in the present situation of the country, and the extreme scarcity of money, for tho' there is such a pother made by some of our *Patriots* about paper money, I think the day is not very far distant when they will be glad to rake and scrape every tattered bill they can lay their hands on. * * *

Your affect. humble servt

RO. C. NICHOLAS.[1]

---

[1] Robert Carter Nicholas was the son of George Nicholas, M.D., who came from England, and married a widow Burwell, of Gloucester county. He was distinguished as a lawyer, as a patriot during the revolution, and as treasurer of the state. He and his wife Anna, daughter of Col. Wilson Cary, were noted for their Christian culture.

MATTHEW CAMPBELL TO GEO. W. FAIRFAX.

ALEXANDRIA, Nov'r 11th, 1773.

Sir:

By this opportunity I send for Mrs Fairfax one box citron which I imported for her from Madeira. * * * * All your relations so far as I at present recollect are well. We have had a prodigious sickly fall, and have lost about forty inhabitants amongst whom was Mr Tom our Presbyterian Minister, his mother, and Mr Joseph Watson. I hope this will find you both happy, in much ease, with society and books. This seems to be the most the world can bestow. Mr Adams joins me in compliments to both and I am with real respect Sir

Your most ob't humb. serv't
MATTHEW CAMPBELL.

---

He left five sons, one of whom, Wilson Cary Nicholas, was an officer in the revolution, a member of the convention to frame the constitution of United States, senator of the United States from 1799 to 1804, and governor of Virginia from 1814 to 1817.

Another son, John, was a member of congress from Virginia from 1793 to 1801. Removed to Geneva, N. Y., and member of the senate of that state from 1806 to 1809.

COL. GEO. F. MERCER TO GEO. W. FAIRFAX.

LONDON, December 2nd, 1773.

My dear Sir:

If this letter should break in upon your retirement I pray you Sir to allow the subject to plead an apology and I am sure it will, as my interest and the furtherance of some of my schemes are dependent upon it. Perhaps you thought, I am sure you wished, that all my Vandalia [1] prospects, were ere this fully within my grasp, but my ill stars still prevail against me. I am not yet Governor, and a fresh objection, the last I hope they have to offer, has arisen against the policy of the grant, so far as it relates to Britain. It is urged that Colonel Fairfax a gentleman lately arrived from Vir-

---

[1] In 1749, Thomas Lee and others of Virginia, with Mr. Hanbury, a London merchant and Quaker, was incorporated as the Ohio company, and obtained a grant of land west of the mountains and south of the Ohio. After Lee's death, Lawrence, brother of George Washington, became principal manager. The Ohio company at length united with Walpole and others, and in 1770 Thomas Walpole, banker of London, Benjamin Franklin, John Sargeant, and Samuel Wharton, petitioned for a separate government of that part of Virginia, south of the Ohio, and west of a certain longitude.

ginia, has confirmed what Lord Hillsborough had suggested, "that the inhabitants of Vandalia were not only out of reach of the arms, but the commerce of Great Britain," and that Colonel Fairfax had said many thousand "families were settled within the bounds of the new Province, and that each of them had a loom and spinning wheel, and would always manufacture every article of cloath they wanted, of course would not want any British manufactures: and that the people on the Ohio might be easily and conveniently governed by Virginia, which not only made the establishment of a new and separate government totally unnecessary, but that the separation of the intended government from that of Virginia under which it was at present, and by whom they were governed, would occasion great murmurs and perhaps insurrections among the settlers."

I do not presume my dear Sir to oppose my own opinion to one so well informed as I am sure you are, and did I suspect you thought what was *reported* to have been your declaration, it would certainly have great weight in future with me, and indeed would, with as much decency as was practicable, retract what really has hitherto been my opinion. I must however pay that respect to the opinion I have hitherto maintained, to suppose this *report* has been spread as coming from one of your knowledge and authority in Virginia, in order to support Lord Hillsborough's assertions, and I am the more persuaded to this, as I recollect you were so obliging as to mention some conversation you had with Mr Pownall, in which you desired you might not be called before any public Board, being in no way interested, and having no knowledge of the dispute between Pennsylvania, Maryland, and the Vandalians about the boundaries of the Provinces, and that you should have stepped forth, justified as you thought you were in your public character to have asserted the claims, and ask redress of the injuries, if any had been offered to Virginia. I beg your pardon, my dear Sir, for presuming to give you this trouble, and I know public justice as well as your friendship manifested to me on so many occasions, will plead my excuse for asking your answer to this letter.

My best wishes attend Mrs Fairfax, and I am with the utmost sincerity my dear Sir
Your much obliged friend and obedient servant
GEO. F. MERCER.[1]

---

HON. JOHN TAYLOE[2] TO GEO. WM. FAIRFAX.

MOUNT AIRY, Dec. 14th, 1773.

Dear Sir:

Altho' I did not intend (by letter at a time when you must have felt anxiety at parting with so many friends) my good wishes yet they accompany you with the sincerity of a real friendship.

Accept now dear friend the hearty congratulations of a friend on your safe passage. * * *

---

[1] Col. George Mercer was an officer in the British service, son of John Mercer, native of Ireland, a resident of Stafford county, and a lawyer of eminence.

[2] William Tayloe came from London to Virginia in 1650. His descendant, the writer of the above letter, was the founder of Mount Airy in Lunenburgh parish, Richmond county. He was member of the first council under the state constitution, and died April 12, 1779, leaving twelve children.

His only son, John, in 1792, married a daughter of Governor Ogle of Maryland, and their eldest son, John, distinguished himself as an officer of the United States navy.

The little son we have is now ill with a cold. * * * * * I have often wished him as happy as his cousin Frank Corbin is, under your care, lest he become a racer for he is fond now of horses to distraction. Indeed his father is foolishly so, for he cannot help wishing for a good nag to take some of the Jockey club plates at Annapolis or Fredericksburg, where a week's sport is establishing for five years upon the principles of the Annapolis. I cannot leave this subject without giving you an historical account of the performance of my old horse Yorick (now 13 years old) who you know has been a stud horse six years. A match was made on him by some young Fauntleroys,[1] against a breed horse of Doctor W<sup>m</sup> Flood's for £500 a side, quite on the Doctor's own terms to run one heat of five miles 12 stone, 12 lbs, which Yorick run easy in 12 minutes and 27 seconds hand in hand the whole way, but what is extraordinary in this is that Yorick could

---

[1] The Fauntleroys are of French origin, and were early settlers on the Rappahannock. William died in 1684, and left three sons: William, Moore, and John, whose descendants are numerous. A young Fauntleroy was killed at the battle of Monmouth, N. J., in June, 1777.

not stand training for bad feet, which was his disorder when Selim beat him being the only time he ever lost the victory, and had not had a regular sweat in eight weeks.[1] This may be amusing to Capt Wentworth or some of your sporting acquaintances, as it must be thought by them a very extraordinary instance in the running way. * * * *

    Your most obed't humble serv't
          JOHN TAYLOE.

---

J. H. NORTON TO GEO. W. FAIRFAX.

      YORK [VA], March 27, 1774.

Dear Sir:

I have by Capt H Esten received your favor of the 27th November, referring me to one by the Nelly, Capt Greig which I have not received and fear has miscarried. I consider myself very fortunate as having been the instrument of rendering your stay and good Mrs Fairfax's

---

[1] *The Pennsylvania Gazette*, August 3, 1774, copies the following from a Virginia paper:

" A CARD.— A Virginian presents his compliments to the Jockey Clubs of Fredericksburg and Portsmouth, and begs

in London, any way agreeable. My father and mother are never so happy as when they can show civilities to my friends from this continent. The affair of inoculation proved quite agreeable to my wishes, a mere bagatelle, and Mrs Fairfax I find surmounted with great fortitude every dread which crowds upon the mind. * * * Tom was at the time of writing to me settling your household in the City of York which from all accounts is a most desirable place, and a comfortable recess you must find it after having passed so many years in this country. I had a very good account of your petit maitre, Mr Corbin which I was glad to hear. I lately heard from your friends in Frederick, Hampton, and Williamsburgh who were all well, as was the family at Laneville. My wife joins me in duty to yourself and Mrs Fairfax. With

---

that they will suppress their sporting spirit, till the circumstances of America, can permit it with more decency. He also begs leave to recommend to the most serious consideration of these Clubs, whether their purses applied to the relief of the distressed Bostonians, would not afford them more real pleasure than all that can arise from viewing a painful contest, between two or three animals."

compliments to Master Corbin I am as ever
Dear Sir

    Your very much obliged
      and most obed't servant
           J. H. NORTON.[1]

Mr Custis[2] is lately married to a lady in Maryland.

---

RICHARD CORBIN TO GEO. W. FAIRFAX.
           LANEVILLE, 27th June, 1774.
Dear Sir:

\*   \*   \*   \*   \*   \*   \*

Two letters I have lately received from Mr Athawes, have given my wife some uneasiness. He tells me Frank[3] is volatile and too much of

---

[1] John Hatley Norton, son of John Norton of London. Rev. John H. Norton was a descendant.

[2] John Parke Custis was the step-son of George Washington. While in charge of a tutor at Annapolis, Md., he fell in love with the second daughter of Benjamin (usually called Benedict) Calvert and engaged himself. Washington objected on account of his youth. He then was sent to King's College, New York city, but returning for the Christmas holidays was soon married. He was an aid-de-camp of Washington at Yorktown, and died at the close of the war at the house of Mr. Basset of Eltham.

[3] See page 137.

a man to be subject to school rules, and that he was afraid of his falling into the dissipation and vices of the times, and that he must either go to the University, or return to Virginia. * * * The Act of Parliament respecting Boston arrived here at the meeting of the Assembly. The part they acted was such that the Governor thought himself obliged to dissolve them. This dissolution as I think is always the case, has inflamed the minds of the people to a greater degree then when the Stamp Act took place, and they seem more determined.[1] As the Assembly did no business, the Fee Bill is expired and the County Courts will do no business, and every thing is in confusion. The Indians are committing devastations in the upper part. Several skirmishes have happened. God knows how these things will end. The Council have

---

[1] The assembly was in session at Williamsburgh, when the news of the Boston port bill arrived. Jefferson and others " rummaged over the pages of Rushworth, and cooked up a resolution" appointing June 1st as a day of fasting and prayer. The day but one after this, the governor dissolved the assembly. Eighty-nine members then met at the Apollo tavern, and pledged cooperation, and recommended an annual congress of delegates from each colony.

prevailed with the Governor to try another Assembly. Writs are issued returnable the 11 Aug'st. The best wishes of all my family wait on you and good Mrs Fairfax and I am with the most sincere regard

Your most obed't humble servant
RD. CORBIN.

---

J. H. NORTON TO GEO. W. FAIRFAX.

YORK TOWN, June 31, 1774.
Dear Sir:

\* \* \* \* \*

I find you wave politicks altogether. The deadly machinations of the ministry against us, must in time lessen our esteem for Great Britain. In consequence of the proceedings at Boston, our colony intend to second their schemes by entering into violent Associations. The late Representatives in our Assembly are to convene on the 1st of August next,[1] when such

---

[1] Convention met and appointed Peyton Randolph, R. H. Lee, Washington, Patrick Henry, Richard Bland, Benj. Harrison and E. Pendleton, delegates to first congress to meet in Philadelphia, in September. A gentleman writing to a friend, notices their arrival there in these words:

"The Virginia delegates to the Congress have arrived in

measures will be adopted as are likely to produce good effects. The Fee Bill is expired and of course no Courts can be held, so that the whole trade of the colony must decline. I wish for better times for they are very much wanted. Your niece Sally Norton and her little girl very well. S. N joins me in duty to you and Mrs Fairfax.

Your very much obliged<br>
and humble servant<br>
J. H. NORTON.

---

SAMUEL ATHAWES TO GEO. W. FAIRFAX.

LONDON, 25th February, 1775.

Dear Sir:

\*    \*    \*    \*    \*

There is a talk of a conciliating plan, but I see myself no appearance of it at present I profess, for there is now a Bill passing the House respecting the fishery so full of cruelty and oppression that it cannot be read by any one who has a spark of humanity, without horror

---

town — they are a fine set of fellows — even the New England men, are milksops to them." — *Reed's Philomathean Address.*

OF AMERICA. 151

and emotion. Five provinces I think because part of one has been thought fit to be declared in rebellion are to be starved for the North Colonies grow but little. They are inhibited by this Bill from receiving any from their sister colonies, nor can they [torn] without a license which I think is only to be granted if they subscribe a certain test and acquiescence to all the measures which has caused all the dispute so that the trade is not only to be demolished, but they are deprived of fish for their subsistence. God knows how this will end, but I heartily wish it may not ruin both countries.

I am with affection Dear Sir
   Your very obed't servant
     SAM'L ATHAWES.

    LONDON, 15th May, 1775.
Dear Sir:
  \*  \*  \*  \*  \*

The Secretary's son Mr John Nelson,[1] Carter Burwell, and Mr Prentice arrived some months

---

[1] Thomas Nelson, son of Scotch Tom of Yorktown, was long secretary of the council, and had three sons in the army of the revolution.

since, the former for their health, and the latter I believe to attend to the practice of our courts of law, and I find them all agreeable young men.[1] Nelson's disorder arose from a strain and was a chirurgical case of which he is recovered, and he and Mr Prentice have engaged their passage with Capt Mitchell who I understand will sail in about seven or eight days. Mr Burwell[1] was this day inoculated being returned from Bristol where he has been by Dr Fothergill's advice for two or three months drinking the waters and living on vegetable diet. There is a Mrs Brodeau[2] who is recommended to me as an accomplished woman skilled in French etc and all kinds of work, of a most sober disposition and good character who is going to New York in order to set up a Boarding School. If you could send a few lines, in a few days, under cover to me, addressed to any one

---

[1] Carter Burwell, son of Lewis, president of the council of Virginia.

[2] On a map of Virginia, prepared near this time, a few miles south of Essex Court House is marked Broder's School, can it be intended for Brodeau?

in that province, by way of introduction to her it would oblige me.

I am with esteem Dear Sir

Your very obed't & obliged serv't

SAM'L ATHAWES.

Col. Phil Lee[1] is no more.

His friend and neighbor George Washington naturally became the agent to attend to the pecuniary concerns of Hon. Geo. W. Fairfax, after he went to England.

In 1774 the plantation of Belvoir was leased to the Rev. Andrew Morton for seven years. The mansion house was brick, two stories in height. Upon the first floor were four rooms and a large hall, and on the second floor were five rooms. In the basement was a servant's hall, and cellar. Convenient offices, stables and coach house adjoined. The garden was large and filled with valuable fruit trees. A few years after, the house was burned.

In examining the following account rendered by Washington, a charge will be noticed for

---

[1] Col. Phil. Lee, father-in-law of Major Gen. Henry Lee, see page 112.

lettering a pew in Pohick church. This edifice is in Truro parish, Fairfax county. It was built of brick from plans drawn by Washington, and completed in 1773, and here worshiped the patriot, George Mason, as well as George Washington. In February, 1773, Washington bought a pew for Geo. W. Fairfax, and gave a bond for £16, and in August, 1774, it was lettered. At the breaking out of the civil war in 1861, the initials G. W. F., were visible.

This was the final account rendered by Washington; for immediately on his appointment to the command of the American army he wrote to Geo. W. Fairfax, that it would be impracticable for him to longer continue to perform the duties of a friend, by having an eye to the conduct of his collector and steward.

OF AMERICA. 155

| Dr. | The Honble Geo. W. Fairfax, Esq., in acct. with Geo. Washington. | | | | | | Cr. |
|---|---|---|---|---|---|---|---|
| 1774 | | | | | 1774 | | |
| June | To Blank Bonds and Bills for your Sale at Belvoir | £0 | 5 | 0 | June 15 | By Ball. of last acc't render'd | £1 8 4½ |
| 29 | To cash sent to the Annapolis printer advertizing Belvoir and the sale of goods there | 2 | 8 | 0 | 18 | By 5 pr ct gain'd in the Contra Bill of Excha: it being had from Colo Syme, at 25 p'r c't instead of 30 p'r c't | 10 0 0 |
| Aug't 15 | To Ditto p'd Wm. Copan putting your cypher (3 letters) on y'r Pew in Polick church at 5s a letter | 15 | 0 | | | By cash p'd Colo Lewis by Littleton Savage on acc't of Giles Cook's Rent | 50 0 0 |
| October | To the Pens'a Gazette advert'g Belv'r to be let | 6 | 5 | | Aug't 17 | By ditto rec'd from Doct'r Craik for a Wilton Carpet bought at your sale in August | 8 10 0 |
| Nov'r 30 | To an express to L'd Fairfax concerning his Renting Belvoir | 6 | 0 | 0 | 23 | By ditto rec'd from Adam Lynn for sundries bought at Ditto | 18 0 0 |
| | To Smith's acc't | 1 | 6 | | Dec'r 17 | By Ditto rec'd Francis Willis for sundries sold at Belvoir y'e 5th inst. | 9 4 9 |
| | | 4 | 1 | 11 | | By Ditto rec'd from Abednego Adams for a pair of scales sold at Do Do | 10 0 0 |
| | | | | | 20 | By cash rec'd from Mr. Craven Peyton p'r acc't sent | 162 2 7½ |
| | To Ball. due and Cred'd pr Contra | 238 | 11 | 10 | | | £242 13 9 |
| | | £242 | 13 | 9 | | By Ball pr Contra | £238 11 10 |
| | | | | | | E. Excepted p'r G'o WASHINGTON |
| | | | | | | April 6th 1775. |

GEO. SHAW TO GEO. W. FAIRFAX.

WOMERSLEY, 20th June, 1775.

Sir:

\*   \*   \*   \*   \*

I am almost afraid to make enquiries about my friends in Virginia, of whom I have heard no tidings for a long season, and indeed I am too much in their debt to expect it. Sorry I am that affairs in the western World have taken so unfavorable a turn, and that any blood should have been drawn in the quarrel. I hop'd our disputes would have been previously adjusted, and tho' this has not fallen out to my wish, I still hope the day is not far off when we shall be bless'd with the joyful news, that both sides have made some healing concessions and re-settled peace on a firm basis. I see nothing to hinder this, if the inflammatory patriots on both sides of the water are not in the way, who with all their zeal may perhaps have the real good of both countries less at heart, than men of fewer pretensions, and greater moderation. It would give me the truest pleasure to hear that you are pursuing measures towards effecting an accommodation between the contending parties.

You cannot engage in a nobler work, nor could I wish you a more honorable inscription in future, than the Saviour of England and America.

I shall take it, as a particular favour, if you will be so kind as to inform me how they do in James and Yorktown, and if you can further tell me on good grounds that you entertain great hopes of a speedy reconciliation between perhaps an obstinate mother and her pert children, I shall be extremely indebted to you. I beg my humble compliments to Mrs Fairfax. My wife desires to add hers. I am with great respect and regard

Your most obd't & obliged servant

GEO. SHAW.[1]

---

SAMUEL ATHAWES TO GEO. W. FAIRFAX.

LONDON, 19th July, 1775.

Dear Sir:

\*          \*          \*          \*          \*

The following extract of a letter which I have received from Virginia, may perhaps ac-

---

[1] Rev. George Shaw of England married a sister of Richard Ambler of Yorktown, and she was the grandmother of Charles Shaw Lefevre, late speaker of the House of Commons of Great Britain.

count for L'd D——e[1] embarking with his family:

"An unfortunate affair happened by some of the citizens assembling at the magazine in order to arm themselves with the guns that were lodged there, and in going in they found two guns planted with spring locks, one of which went off and wounded three men, one dangerously, one lost two fingers, the other but slightly. The trap was laid by the G——r which has incensed the people amazingly against him.[2] It's imagined the Assembly will take it under consideration to-morrow, and how it will end God knows."

\*　　\*　　\*　　\*　　\*

Yours very affectionately<br>Sam'l Athawes.

---

[1] Lord Dunmore.

[2] The next day, June 6th, Gov. Dunmore and family escaped from Williamsburg to return no more, and took shelter on board the man of war Fowey.

NATHANIEL TUCKER TO GEO. W. FAIRFAX.

EDINBURGH, 11th Sept'r, 1775.

Dear Sir :

\*    \*    \*    \*    \*

Should Lady Dundas be so obliging as to re-remember the offer she made of giving me letters to some of her friends here, they will arrive safe under your care if directed to me at the Reverend D<sup>r</sup> Blacklocks, Bristo Street Edinburgh. I have good lodgings and am settled much to my satisfaction here in an agreeable and sober family in the suburbs not far from College, but sequestered from the noise and other disagreeable circumstances, that attend a residence in the city. But alas, my dear Sir, I do not find that the people here interest themselves in favor of our unhappy country, like those in Yorkshire.

Few, very few are the friends we find among them and I am kept so much in the dark with regard to transactions abroad that any information in that respect would be a treat to me. Never since I crossed the Atlantic have I received a line from any of my friends either on the continent or in Bermuda, a circumstance which gives me a great deal of uneasiness and preys much upon my spirits. But it boots not to complain. * * * * *

Your very affectionate humb. serv't

NAT TUCKER.[1]

---

STEPHEN CROFT TO GEO. W. FAIRFAX.

YORK, [Eng.] Oct'r 1st, 1775.

Dear Sir:

I am very much obliged to you for a copy of the letter from Bunker Hill,[2] and dare say the

---

[1] The second wife of the elder Thomas Nelson of Yorktown was a widow Tucker, whose first husband was from Bermuda.

Nat and St. George Tucker were brothers, and the latter, during the revolution, lived in the Bermudas.

Henry St. George Tucker, son of St. George, was born in 1779, and married the mother of John Randolph of Roanoke. He was sometimes called the Virginia Blackstone, and was president of the Virginia court of appeals, and a congressman from Virginia from 1815 to 1819. He died at Winchester, 1828.

[2] Reference is made to the following letter of Washington, which is copied from Sparks:

"CAMP AT CAMBRIDGE, 25 July, 1775.

"Dear Sir: On the other side you will receive a copy of my last, dated at Philadelphia, the 31st of May, and to which I refer. I shall say very little in this letter, for two

account is a true one notwithstanding what we have heard to the contrary. Every man's natural wish must be for that man, or body who is determined to support his liberty rather then become an abject slave, but you and I have lived to see that venality and corruption damp that Isle which formerly gloried in being

---

reasons; first, because I have received no letter from you since the one dated in June, 1774, and therefore, having written often, can have nothing to answer; but principally because I do not know, whether it may ever get to your hands. If it should, the principal, indeed only design, is to cover the second of three bills forwarded in my last. You will, I presume, before this letter gets to hand, hear of my appointment to the command of the Continental army. I arrived at this camp, the 2d inst.

" You must no doubt, also have heard of the engagement on Bunker's Hill, the 17th ultimo; but as I am persuaded, you will have a very erroneous account transmitted of the loss sustained on the side of the Provincials. I do assure you, upon my word, that our loss as appears by the returns, made to me, since I came here, amounts to no more than one hundred and thirty-nine killed, thirty-six missing, and two hundred and seventy-eight wounded; nor had we, if I can credit the most solemn assurances of the officers who were in the action, above one thousand five hundred men engaged on that day.

" The loss on the side of the Ministerial troops, as I am informed from good authority, consisted of one thousand and forty-three killed and wounded, whereof ninety-two were officers."

a Protector, and see addresses desiring a Court and Ministry to go all lengths, who were sufficiently inclined to run every risk, rather than give up their darling scheme of tyranny, and orlorn as the situation may be of those who act upon true Whig principles, yet I trust they will boldly bear their testimony of their disapprobation of the dire effects of this mad and wicked project which proceeds from genuine Toryism, but it's somewhat hard to bear under the Brunswick line, and to hear the pretence of zeal and affection, but I hope in some cool hour some honest good man may be found to stop the effusion of blood and treasure which seems to threaten, and must happen to the mother and children if carried on much longer.

This is my prayer: *Peace with just and equal liberty*, but violence is the word at present. I beg but compliments to your Lady.

Your most obliged and<br>
most ob't humble servt<br>
STEPH<sup>N</sup> CROFT.[1]

---

[1] Stephen Croft, a prominent citizen of Yorkshire, grandfather of Rev. James Croft, archdeacon of Canterbury.

NAT. TUCKER TO GEO. W. FAIRFAX.

EDINBURGH, Oct. 23d, 1775.

Dear Sir:

\*   \*   \*   \*   \*

I thank you for the kind hint for your good opinion of my prudence in avoiding to make myself enemies among the sticklers for Party. I do assure you, my dear Sir, you oblige me very much by the extract you give me from the letter of your illustrious correspondent.[1] It afforded me vast satisfaction because it leaves room to judge what kind of opposition is likely to be made by the Americans to the British troops the fame of whose glorious achievments has been extended throughout the known world. It likewise shows us how little credit is to be given to common report which generally receives its complexion from the crooked and foul channel thro' which it passes. I have lately received letters from Bermuda dated 5th August, and among them one from my brother St George, who is gone to exercise his profession in our little Island 'till the happy time shall arrive

---

[1] See letter of Washington, date Cambridge, July 25, 1775, on page 157.

when the restoration of peace to the Continent shall enable him to return and settle there. I am glad to find that the patriotic county of Middlesex has been exerting itself in opposition to the measures of a corrupt Administration. God grant that its effort may be crowned with success.

Your obliged & affectionate humble serv't<br>
NAT TUCKER.

---

HON. ROBERT FAIRFAX TO GEO. W. FAIRFAX.

LEEDS CASTLE, 20th Nov., 1775.

Dear Sir:

Yesterday I received a letter from our friend Mr John Randolph,[1] your Attorney General.

---

[1] John Randolph, attorney general, was son of Hon. John Randolph, speaker of the house of burgesses, who died in 1737, and grandson of William of Turkey island, James river, who came from England in 1660, and by industry and intelligence amassed a large estate.

He was also brother of Peyton Randolph, president of the first Continental congress. Sympathizing with Lord Dunmore and the tory party, John Randolph went to England, and died in London in 1784, aged fifty-six.

His son Edmund stayed in Virginia, and was an aid to General Washington, member of congress, one of the framers of the constitution of the United States, attorney general of the United States, and secretary of state.

He wrote from Rochester in his way from the coast to London, with his lady and two daughters.

He informs me that my Brother was extremely ill and that Col Stephens had no hopes of his recovery, nature being quite worn out.[1] I thought proper to let you know this and wish you would not mention any thing about my brother, till we hear more. I am

Yours affectionately<br>R. FAIRFAX.

---

EDWARD, LORD HAWKE TO GEO. W. FAIRFAX.

SUNBURY, MIDDLESEX, 30th Nov$^{br}$, 1775.

Dear Sir:

I have received a very fine large Salmon, which arrived safe, in perfect order, and good condition. By the direction I apprehend it must come from you, and therefore beg you will permit me to return you my most hearty thanks

---

[1] Thomas, sixth Lord Fairfax, then at Greenway Court named after an ancestral seat in England. During the revolution he adhered to the royal cause, and according to tradition, mortification from the surrender of Cornwallis at Yorktown, hastened his death in 1782. Robert was his successor to the title.

for it, as I must confess it is the finest fish I have seen of a long while.

I was extremely sorry that my time would not permit me to pay my respects to you and Mrs Fairfax before I left Yorkshire, for being an invalid and doubtful of the weather, made me anxious to get home as soon as possible. I shall flatter myself, my good Sir, with the hopes of seeing you with Mrs Fairfax at my house at Sunbury, and altho' a cottage, the Master will receive you with a cheerful countenance, and you will find a hearty welcome. I cannot expect this favor, unless you should come into the South (as the distance is so far) but then I shall hope you will give me that pleasure. I must beg you will present my respectful compliments with those of Miss Birt to Mrs Fairfax, and that you will believe me to be with the highest esteem and regard. My dear Sir

Your most obedient and

most humble servant

E. HAWKE.[1]

---

[1] Sir Ed. Hawke's mother was sister of Colonel Martin Bladen, and thus connected with Mr. Fairfax. In 1765 Hawke was made vice admiral of the Blue, and in 1776 was created Baron Hawke.

REV: JONATHAN BOUCHER TO GEO. W. FAIRFAX.

LONDON, Dec. 15th, 1775.

Sir:

I take the liberty by this opportunity by Mr Clapham,[1] the eldest son of your friend of that name in Annapolis, to enquire after yours and Mrs Fairfax's welfare. I left America that unhappy scene of trouble and confusion, about the latter end of September along with the Rev Mr Addison,[2] his son, and my wife who all request to be affectionately remembered to you.

This young man who is himself very worthy, and for whose father, I have long had the greatest regard, is somewhat embarrassed how to dispose of himself. Mr Hanbury to whom he was more particularly recommended, and who has taken

---

[1] The son of Jo. Clapham of Annapolis, clerk of the revenue board of the province.

[2] Rev. Henry Addison, A.M., was the son of Thomas Addison, a member of the council, and grandson of Col. John Addison, surveyor general of the province of Maryland, who built Oxon Hall below Washington city on the Potomac, which still stands. He was educated at Queen's College, Oxford, and in 1751, married Rachel, daughter of the celebrated lawyer, Daniel Dulany of Annapolis. He was rector of St. John's parish, Prince George county, Md. A tory in sentiment, he went to England at the commence-

very obliging and friendly notice of him, could he says, he believes with no very great trouble get him into a Counting House here. But the wages of such an appointment are so inconsiderable, and the prospect of his hereafter getting forward with advantage in the world, in this way, so very little encouraging that he seems to think it can be eligible only to those who can do nothing else. Now this young gentleman, has already got some share of classical learning, and is said to have an exceedingly fine capacity for making a proficiency in the Classics. Mr Hanbury is therefore talking with me on the subject, appeals to me whether there was not a greater probability of his doing well by pursuing his studies in that way than by attempting

---

ment of the revolution, but in 1780 returned to New York city, and wrote to General Washington for permission to go to Maryland, but the request was not granted. After peace was declared, he came to the home of his ancestors, and died in 1789, aged about seventy-two years. In 1786, the legislature of Maryland allowed his son to hold certain lands that had been confiscated. He owned the tract opposite the Washington Navy Yard, at the junction of the Anacostan, the Indian name of the eastern branch, with the Potomac, upon a portion of which the writer resides. In the mansion of my neighbor, Mr. Anthony Addison, is a fine portrait of Rev. Henry Addison and wife.

the mercantile department. To the accomplishment of this however, money will be necessary, and I am fearful the little sum his father was on the instant able to give him may be quite inadequate to the expense of going thro' even a school education.

He has an Aunt in Tadcaster, where it is said there is a good school and as she is at least convenient, I would fain flatter myself it may be in her power to accommodate him for a year or two, till haply the dark cloud now hanging over America, may be dispersed, and his father have it in his power to make him some remittances. \* \* \* \* \*

Your most obl'gd & most h'ble servt
JONA<sup>N</sup> BOUCHER.[1]

---

[1] Rev. Jonathan Boucher, born in 1738, was one of the ablest divines of the church of England in America. He came to Virginia at an early age, taught school in Port Royal, and was rector of Hanover parish, King George. From thence he went to St. Mary's parish in Caroline county. His next charge was at Annapolis, Maryland, and there John Parke Custis, step-son of General Washington, was his pupil.

His last parish was Queen Anne's, in Prince George county. He had been opposed to the stamp act, but at length sustained the cause of the mother country, and became very unpopular. In his farewell sermon, he says: " It was my misfortune to be first known to you in these unsettled times.

### JOHN NORTON TO GEO. W. FAIRFAX.

LONDON, the 6th January, 1776.

Dear Sir:

I wish I could give you any agreeable news from Virginia, but every thing seems to be growing worse and worse. Mr Benj. Johnston that formerly lived in Fredericksburg is here, one of the last from thence; he left Virginia 22nd Oct. Mr John Baylor[1] is likewise arrived

---

Pains were taken to prejudice you against me even before you saw me. Many of you must remember, as I for ever shall, how on coming to take possession of my living the doors were shut * * * * nor can you have forgotten how near I was, on that memorable day, experiencing the fate of Stephen." Ejected from his parish he went back to England.

In 1795, while vicar of Epsom, he published thirteen discourses preached in America, between 1763 and 1775, and dedicated the work to George Washington. He devoted the latter years of his life in preparing a *Glossary of Provincial and Archæological Words.*

His wife was Miss Addison of Addison's Manor, near the present site of Washington city. Descendants still live on the original tract.

[1] John Baylor, the first of the name in Virginia arrived in 1650, and settled in Gloucester county.

John, the third of the name, married Lucy Walker at Yorktown, January 2, 1744, and a sister of Lucy Walker married John Norton of London, England, the writer of the above letter.

The fourth John Baylor was born at New Market, Caro-

in Scotland but not yet come to London, I have had a letter from him. Mr John Randolph, his lady and two daughters have been at our next door neighbour's Campbell's when Mrs Necks took lodgings for them. The ladies have gone thro' the small pox and are now removed to the other end of the town. The Philadelphia papers speak of a skirmish that has happened between Capt Squires of one of the tenders at Hampton, and some of the Militia commanded by Capt Nicholas (suppose our friend's son) and Capt Lyne in which they beat off the men of war's people, and killed several of their hands without loss to themselves.[1] It is said tho' I know not with what truth that Commissioners are to go with the intended Army which is to consist of 50,000 men. God send that peace and tranquillity may once more ensue, tho' I

---

line county, Sept. 4, 1750, at twelve years of age was sent to Putney grammer school, England. He married in England his cousin Fanny, daughter of John Norton of London, and returned to Virginia.

Mrs. Baylor's brother John H. Norton, also resided in Virginia.

[1] Dunmore threatened to burn Hampton in retaliation, but he was at length driven off, by a party sent from Williamsburg.

must own there is but a poor prospect of that event happening soon. The thoughts of it depresses my spirits as well as those of my family who join in me best wishes to yourself and lady.

Your very obed't servant<br>JOHN NORTON.

---

GEO. W. FAIRFAX TO JOHN NORTON.

Dear Sir:

\*   \*   \*   \*   \*   \*   \*

I was very soon informed of Mr Randolph's arrival and must own I was never more astonished, but did not hear of Mr Baylors until the receipt of yours. I presume the latter is come over on acc't of his health, or some business of consequence, but I am afraid the former's coming forbodes no good to his country, and I shall not be surprised if I should see in the papers his appointment to some lucrative place here. I really pity and sympathize with those that were here before these unhappy disputes commenced, and now reside in England whose chief dependence was in having regular remittances from that once happy country Virginia, that will shortly become one of the principal seats of war.

I cannot believe that the Ministry will be able to get 50,000 men landed in America, or that the Commissioners will do any thing effectual, unless they are allowed to treat with the Continental Congress. They may indeed protract matters, and enrich themselves with the overflowing of your T—y, but I expect very little national advantage from their negotiations. However I do sincerely and most heartily wish, that I may be disappointed, and that the Commissioners may obtain peace and tranquillity throughout the British Dominions, tho' from letters lately received from G. W———[1] I must agree with you, there is but very little prospect of so happy an event. Sad reflections for me, my good Sir, whose chief resources are now cut off, and forced to contract his living to the small income he has here    *    *    *    *

Your most obedient and very humble servant

G. W. FAIRFAX.

---

[1] G. W. George Washington.

### SAMUEL ATHAWES TO GEO. W. FAIRFAX.

LONDON, 9th Feb'y, 1776.

Dear Sir:

\* \* \* \* \* \* \*

It has often been reported that Quebec is taken but I do not believe it; however I saw a gentleman who was just come to town from New York, and he says it was correctly reported that Lord Dunmore had given directions (for it is said he was not in the action himself) for the negroes, indentured servants, and about 80 Grenadiers in all about 600, to attack about 1000 Virginians and North Carolinians in their intrenchments, and that the assailants were not only repulsed, but in a manner cut to pieces. It is said his Lordship I think was induced to this by some information in which he was deceived.[1] The preparations making here are surely sufficient to make a humane man shudder,

---

[1] At an early hour, before sunrise on Dec. 9, 1775, Capt. Fordyce marched the British troops over the causeway, on the north side of the Elizabeth River, at the Great Bridge, and assaulted the Americans. Fordyce and every Grenadier was killed. Lord Dunmore was induced to make the attack by the false representations from a servant lad, who had deserted from the American camp.

and under these circumstances would it not be more becoming us as a Nation by fasting and prayer to the Almighty to omit the impending calamity than by dissipating at masquerades, regattas, etc.

I am with truth Dear Sir
Your affectionate & obliged serv't
SAM$^L$ ATHAWES.

---

BIOGRAPHICAL NOTICE OF REV. BRYAN, EIGHTH LORD FAIRFAX.

Bryan Fairfax was the eldest child of Hon. Wm. Fairfax, by his last wife. During the French and Indian war he was in the military service of Virginia, and the following extract from his writings seems to indicate that he became a religious man at that period:

"From twelve at night till two it was my turn to stand sentinel at a dangerous post. I had a fellow sentinel, but I desired him to go away which he willingly did. As soon as I was alone, I kneeled down, and determined not to rise, but to continue crying and wrestling with God, till he had mercy on me."

He married Miss Cary, a sister of his brother

George's wife. In 1765 he went to England, and while there the troubles began in Virginia arising from the Stamp Act. Daniel McCarty an old friend wrote to him on April 27, 1766, relative to a debtor.

"We have had no law to compel him, or any other person to pay any thing, since the first day of last November, all of our Courts from that time being shut up on account of the Stamp Acts."

In a few months he returned to Virginia, and in 1774 in a letter to Washington expressed himself as unfavorable to the resolutions of Fairfax county, relative to the British Government. Lossing says: "Just at the close of a mild April day while he [Washington] and his neighbor, Bryan Fairfax, with Major Gates were discussing the stirring events at Williamsburg connected with the seizure of powder belonging to the colony, by the royal governor, and the bold stand taken by Patrick Henry, a messenger came in haste from Alexandria, bearing intelligence of bloodshed at Lexington and Concord."[1]

---

[1] Mount Vernon and its Associations. p. 98.

Although Mr. Fairfax disapproved of the measures of Parliament, he was opposed to forcible resistance, and in the year 1777 having obtained a passport went to New York to embark for England, but the oath prescribed by the British commander there, was so strict, that he could not conscientiously take it. On his return to Virginia, he again visited Washington, then at Valley Forge, and was received by him with his wonted kindness.[1]

In the year 1789 he became a minister of the Protestant Episcopal church, and was probably ordained by Bishop White. While decided in his preferences for his own branch, he was free from bigotry, and accepted the moderate Calvinistic interpretation of the thirty-nine articles.

As a preacher while not eloquent, he was logical and practical.

An extract from a Sermon occasioned by the death of Rev. David Griffith[1] of Fairfax parish,

---

[1] In Sparks's Correspondence of Washington, vol. 5, p. 246 is a letter of Fairfax, expressing his appreciation of Washington's courtesy, and the reply of the general thereto.

[1] Rev. David Griffith of New York, received orders in England in 1770, and upon his return to America, preached for a short period at Gloucester, New Jersey. Having

and delivered at Fall's church August 16, 1789, and at Alexandria on the succeeding Sunday, from the text "So teach us to number our days, that we may apply our hearts unto wisdom," Ps. 90th. 12 v., will give some idea of his directness in the pulpit.

"But the loss of our friends or relatives or acquaintance will often prove a more powerful means to remind us of our own departure, and so teach us to number our days.

"The Lord gives us many occasions, and many more than we rightly improve. The late mournful occasion may teach us the uncertainty of this life, and how needful it is to be always prepared to die. We have lost our worthy minister of this Parish, and what could be more unexpected? What a loss to his friends! But how great a loss to his family, none but they who are acquainted with it can rightly know.

---

removed to Virginia, he was elected in July, 1776, chaplain of 3d Va. Battalion. In 1786 he was chosen Bishop of the Virginia diocese of the Protestant Episcopal church, but owing to his pecuniary circumstances was not able to go to England for consecration. In 1789 he resigned, and Bishop Madison became his successor. On August 3d he died at the residence of Bishop White in Philadelphia, Pa.

'Tis true they who sympathize with the distressed may conceive in general the situation of a family deprived of its head, and truly pity it. But a loving and well ordered family sustains more than a common loss under its peculiar circumstances. When the head of a family is taken from it at such a time, so far from home and so unexpectedly, so useful and so beloved, (for it is hard to say whether the wife, or children, or father loved most) what shall we say as to the dispensation of Providence, but that his ways are past finding out.

"But as the living know they must die, you should draw a lesson from the sad occasion, and reflect that you know not how soon your time may come. If you know not the time of your departure you should the sooner and more diligently apply your hearts into wisdom.

"If he is to render an account of his ministry, you also are to give an account how you have heard, and what improvement you have made from it. You know he was diligent in his ministry as well as prudent in his deportment. And if any have been too slack in giving that support which they had promised 'tis to be hoped that they will remember their defects, and join the benevolent in their designed relief. 'Tis indeed a duty in the people, to support their minister, for the Lord hath ordained that they which preach the Gospel should live of the Gospel. I need not insist on it, for it is so plain a duty and so reasonable that every one must acknowledge it. But the faults of a congregation must be pointed out or how shall they seek after wisdom?"

The vestry of Fairfax parish, chose Mr. Fairfax to succeed Mr. Griffith, and he continued to be their minister until 1792, when to the regret of the parishioners he resigned.[1]

Washington in a letter to Sir John Sinclair, written on Dec. 11, 1796, makes an interesting statement relative to the old Fairfax plantation, and the family. He says:

"Within full view of Mount Vernon, separated therefrom by water only, is one of the most beautiful seats on the river for sale, but of greater magnitude than you seem to have contemplated.

---

[1] Rev. Bernard Page, before the war, a minister of the church of England in New York, became his successor.

"It is called Belvoir, and belonged to George William Fairfax, who, were he living would now be Baron of Cameron, as his younger brother in this country (George William dying without issue) at present is, though he does not take upon himself the title. The seat was the abovenamed gentleman's before he went to England, and was accommodated with very good buildings, which were burnt soon after he left them. There are near two thousand acres of land belonging to the tract, surrounded in a manner by water. The mansion-house stood on high and commanding ground; the soil is not of the best quality, but a considerable part of it, lying level, may with proper management be properly cultivated. At present it be-belongs to Thomas Fairfax son of Bryan Fairfax the gentleman who as I said before, will not take upon himself the title of Baron of Cameron."

In 1798 the Rev Mr. Fairfax visited England, and proceedings were instituted to determine the validity of his title as Baron of Cameron. He returned to America in 1799, in time to be one of the sincerest mourners at the funeral of his lifelong friend and neighbor, George Washington.

The following are the names of the chief mourners and the order in which they followed the remains of the great good man from the mansion to the tomb at Mount Vernon.

The printed order of procession states the "Principal mourners, namely:

Mrs Stuart and Mrs Law
Miss Nancy and Sally Stuart
Miss Fairfax and Miss Dennison
Mr Law and Mr Peter,
Mr Lear and Dr Craik,
Lord Fairfax and Ferdinando Fairfax."

Washington in his will did not forget his friend, but says " to the Reverend, now Bryan Lord Fairfax I give a Bible in three large folio volumes, with notes, presented to me, by the Right Reverend Thomas Wilson, Bishop of Sodor and Man."

On May 6, 1800, Lord Walsingham made a report to the House of Lords from the committee " appointed to consider the petition of the Rev. Bryan Fairfax to his Majesty, claiming the title and dignity of Lord Fairfax of Cameron," after which it was

"Resolved and adjudged by the Lords spiritual and temporal in Parliament assembled, that the claimant, the Reverend Bryan Fairfax, hath made out his claim to the title and dignity of Lord Fairfax of Cameron."

Mr. Fairfax never assumed the empty title, and in 1802 died at Mount Eagle, near Alexandria, Va.

---

JOSIAS CLAPHAM TO REV. BRYAN FAIRFAX.

Jan. 7, 2nd, 1789.

Sir:

With this you will receive a few lines from Mr Johnson[1] respecting the Falls etc. For my part I have long had an inclination to have water works at the Falls, and notwithstanding the fall in value of lumber, with the great increase of the number of mills in the country I still retain a fondness for that situation and I am of opinion that Mr Lee[2] on due consideration will never possess it, except he can draw

---

[1] Gov. Johnson of Maryland.
[2] General Harry Lee of the revolution was a graduate of Princeton. After the war he was in 1786 a delegate to

you into a more advantageous bargain than the old lease. I am fully satisfied that to bring iron ore down from Kitockton to blow there will not answer, the heavy sum due you and the large annual rent etc. When all these things are duly considered I am of opinion Col. Lee will give it up, but if it should fall out otherwise I doubt not that we shall settle our matter with you on reasonable terms. I am Sir

    Your most obed't servant
      JOSIAS CLAPHAM.

---

Congress, and in 1791 was governor of Virginia. In 1799 he was a member of congress and delivered the Eulogy on Washington, and was the author of the sentence " First in peace, first in war, and first in the hearts of his countrymen." Land speculations about the Falls of the Potomac and other localities impoverished him. He died at Cumberland island, near St Mary's, Georgia, in 1818. Robert E. Lee, president of Washington College, Lexington, Va., is his son.

BISHOP MADISON[1] TO REV. BRYAN FAIRFAX.

Rev'd Sir:

The importance of the office of a visitor in our Church, and the necessity which exists particularly in its present state for the most strict and zealous discharge of the duties required, must I am persuaded be fully known to you. But the neglect of too many of the visitors hitherto has determined me to forward to each an earnest request to be no longer inattentive to the duties prescribed to them by the Canons. Let me then hope that your best and warmest exertions will not be wanting in your District to stimulate both by word and example the laity and clergy to a diligent attention to those duties upon which the interest of religion and the prosperity of our Church so much depends. Let me hope and intreat that you will be particularly attentive to the conduct of the clergy, and that you will hold it as a sacred duty to which every other consideration must

---

[1] Bishop Madison was born in Rockbridge county, Va., 1749, and graduated at William and Mary in 1772. President of the college in 1777, consecrated bishop of Virginia in 1790, by the archbishop of Canterbury.

yield to enforce the Canons wherever a *disregard* or the *least immorality* shall appear.

I flatter myself I shall receive a full and regular report of the state of each parish in your district, on or before the meeting of the next Convention, as I shall then propose, God willing, that all the reports of visitors be read by the Secretary.

I am Rev'd Sir with great respect

Y'r serv't and brother

J. MADISON.

July 10, 1792.

---

BISHOP SEABURY[1] TO REV. BRYAN FAIRFAX.

NEW LONDON, March 1, 1794.

Rev. and Dear Sir:

The last evening Mr Jonathan Starr presented me with 200 dollars, received by him in a letter from you. Greatly was I affected by

---

[1] Samuel Seabury, D.D., was a native of Groton, Ct., born in 1729. Graduated at Yale, and in 1751 went to Edinburgh to study medicine. Subsequently he studied theology and was ordained in 1753 at London, by Bishop Sherlock. During the war of the revolution he sided with Great Britain and resided in New York. Was elected bishop of Connecticut in 1783, and consecrated in 1784 at Aberdeen, Scotland, by Bishop Kilgour.

this your liberality; both as it was a testimony of regard for me, and an instance of the bountiful disposition of your heart, and shews that it delights in works of benevolence and charity. Acceptable to God must that heart be, which imitates the divine goodness in scattering benefits and extending blessings to its fellows. God only can reward you, and his reward is certain—the comfort and satisfaction which ever spring from that faith which worketh by love, and the glorious prospect of that heavenly kingdom, where nothing but love can dwell, must be yours by actual possession, and by sure hope founded in the mediation and through the ever prevalent intercession of Jesus.

Accept my most unfeigned acknowledgments. I wish much to know how you are, and how you get on through this miserable world. The longer I live in it, the more I am convinced that its true worth is only estimated by our holy religion. It is only a passage to a better life, to that life which alone is worthy of the name. God grant we both may find it.

The discourses I formerly mentioned, have been published. I wish to know whether they have reached you. You had a son in Philad$^a$, did I know his direction, it would facilitate my communications to you.

Commending you, and all your concerns to the protection and blessing of Almighty God, I remain your most obliged, and very affectionate, hum. serv$^t$.

     S. B$^p$. Connect, & Rho. Isle.

---

PRESIDENT WASHINGTON TO REV. BRYAN FAIRFAX.

    GERMAN TOWN,[1] Sep. 8$^{th}$, 1794.

My dear Sir:

It is not my wish to add to the trouble which I am sorry has been thrown upon you (in a manner unavoidably) in the management of the suit against the representatives or security of the deceased Doct'r Savage. But when I am written to on this subject by those who are interested therein, I feel the necessity of making some response, lest silence should receive an unfavorable interpretation.

On this ground I give you the trouble of

---

[1] During the sickly season in Philadelphia, the president and other officers of United States government, resided at Germantown, six miles distant.

perusing the enclosed letter from a Mr Peter Trener, and my answer; after which let me pray you to put a wafer in the letter and cause it to be forwarded, agreeably to the superscription, by the first good conveyance that may present itself to your view.

Who Mr Trener is I know not, nor have I any recollection of what he says I wrote to him on the 16$^{th}$ of Nov'r 1786 (having no papers of that date by me, at this place to recur to). I have some imperfect remembrance it is true of an application that was made to me by a person in Virginia about the period he mentions, with which I was not favorably impressed, but why I was not so, or whether it came from this person I am unable to inform you with the least precision, nor is it of much account, as the authenticity and regularity of the papers he alludes to must decide his pretensions.

With best respects to Mrs Fairfax, and with very sincere esteem and regard for yourself I remain Dear Sir

Your most affect$^e$ &<br>
obedient servant<br>
G$^o$ Washington.

The Rev'd Mr Fairfax.

PRESIDENT WASHINGTON TO REV. BRYAN FAIRFAX.

PHILADELPHIA, 3d Jan'y, 1796.

Dear Sir:

Your favor of the 16th ult'o came safe, but not in the time which might have been expected from the date of it.

Mr Davies letter is herewith returned. I do not know that more could have been done, than you have attempted to do; but it is exceedingly to be regretted, that villainy, chicanery, and every species of delay should bring justice in such jeopardy, if it is not entirely defeated by them. I shall hope however that as long there remains a tolerable chance of coming at it, that the suit will be prosecuted, and that Colo' Simms and whoever else is employed therein will exert themselves to the utmost.

I am of opinion that good policy dictates the propriety of assuring them a *handsome* fee, or rather a certain per-centage if they succeed; nothing if they do not.

Trifling fees are thrown away upon lawyers of any eminence, for they excite no exertion; and it cannot be expected that in a case, which is, in a manner desperate, and without any appropriate funds, that large fees can be paid from our private purses. My advances to Mrs Savage in her life, during the days of her distress was pretty considerable, and the Clerk's and Sheriffs fees are continually adding to it. Yours I am persuaded are equal thereto, and together shew the expediency of a vigorous effort; which I see no other means of making than the one I have suggested.

My respects and the compliments of the season, in which Mrs Washington joins me, are offered to Mrs Fairfax and yourself. And with sincere esteem and regard I am Dear Sir

Your most obed't & affect servant

G° Washington.

The Rev'd Mr Fairfax.

---

EARL OF BUCHAN[1] TO REV. LORD FAIRFAX.

DRYBURGH ABBEY, MELROSE, October 10, 1798.

My good Lord:

Having been at my residence in West Lothian when your Lo'p's letter Sept. 27, came to

---

[1] David Stewart Erskine, Lord Cardross, and Earl of Buchan, was the second son of Henry, 10th Earl of that

this place, and that I did not return hither till the 6 inst. I could not sooner with deliberation, give any proper solution to your queries.

With respect to entails in England they can bind no further than to those in life when the settlement in trust is made but can be cut off by fine and recovery, a form or feature of law to defeat them, as you will see explained by Blackstone in his Commentaries on the Laws of England, and in his Analysis. I do not therefore expect that there can remain any actionable claim or any succession of the Lords Fairfax of Cameron.

In relation to my kinsman Charles Lord Fairfax of Emley and Gilling, he was descended from William the 3d son of Thomas the 1st Viscount. I from the $2^d$ whose name was Henry, but Charles married the daughter and

---

name and half brother of Thomas Lord Erskine, Lord Chancellor of England. His mother was Frances, daughter of Henry Fairfax of Hurst. After leaving the university of Glasgow, he proceeded to London, and was an attaché of the Earl of Chatham. He was the chief originator of the society of Antiquaries of Scotland. Owing to declining health in 1787, he moved to Dryburgh Abbey. He contributed various papers to scientific and literary journals, and died in 1829, at an advanced age.

heiress of Nicholas, son of the 2ᵈ visc't, so that he had a good title there being no entail in force to cut him off. At any rate Charles, lived so long that he could make a new settlement in favor of the *Pigots* his nephews, who I find have sold that fine old place of Gilling Castle Manor, which when you happen to be at York again, it would be interesting to look at as a curiosity from its antiquity and beautiful situation.

With respect to the pedigree of your own family, it corresponds to my supposition, and believeing that your Lordship can have no difficulty in proving it legally, you may think it reasonably proper to have your right ascertained to vote as a Peer of Scotland, at their elections, on which I am sure my brother will be ready to advise you as to the least expensive and most proper mode of obtaining the right thereunto, whether by service here in Scotland, or on exhibition of writs or by petition to his Majesty, and a consequent reference to a Committee of the House of Peers.[1]

---

[1] Thomas Lord Erskine was half brother of Earl of Buchan. For four years he was a British midshipman, and

The account your Lo'p gives me of the various disappointments incident to your worthy life move me greatly to reflect upon the circumstances which form as it were a laboratory of virtue, there being nothing more certain than our being profited by difficulties and by sufferings.

In whatever way by my brother's direction, I can be the means of promoting the expectation and establishment of y'r right to the Peerage of Cameron, it will give me great satisfaction, and I beg you will mention to our excellent friend, General Washington, the great pleasure it affords me to co-operate with him in friendship towards y'r Lordship and your family. Being my Good Lord with great regard

>Your wellwishing kinsman

>>and ob. h. serv't

>>>BUCHAN.

---

then served eight years in the army, but in 1777 became a law student of Lincoln's Inn, and in 1778, in the case of Captain Baillie, established his reputation as an eloquent pleader. After the riots of Lord George Gordon of 1780, he protested against the doctrine of constructive treason. In 1783 he became an M. P. In 1792 he defended Thomas Paine, the author of Common Sense, and in 1794 Horne Tooke charged with treason. In 1806 he was made a peer by the title of Lord Erskine, and became chancellor of Great Britain. He died in 1823.

LADY ERSKINE TO REV. BRYAN LORD FAIRFAX.

My Good Lord:

Lest your Lordship should mistake the direction which I gave you in haste last night I send it you in writing, viz: Zion's chapel near White Chapel church. When you come to Zion Chapel, make the coachman draw up to the door at the back part of the Chapel, and enquire for Mr Emerson, who will have pleasure in placing your Lordship in a proper seat. Since I saw you, I have had an opportunity of making a full enquiry on the subject of the pictures, both in water colour or oil, and of the sizes you mentioned, and I think the information I have to give you will be satisfactory.

I hope you caught no cold last night, and are better to-day. I am with sincere regard
    Your Lordships obliged friend
        and humble serv't
            A. A. ERSKINE.[1]

Spa-Fields,
  Octobr 27, 1798.

---

[1] Lady Ann Agnes Erskine was distinguished for piety, and was the trustee of Countess of Huntingdon's chapels. Zion Chapel had been intended for a theatre, but was pur-

### E. MIDDLETON TO BRYAN, LORD FAIRFAX.

KENSINGTON PALACE, Novemb'r 7th.

I shall be very glad of seeing your Lordship on Friday next, and dinner shall be order'd at the hour of Five. I hope to have my two old friends to meet you that day, but poor Sir James Napier is I fear not well enough in this bad cold weather to venture out, and Sir William uncertain. So perhaps you will only find myself, who will be always glad to receive so worthy a friend and relation. I am my Lord

Your Lordships obedient serv't

E. MIDDLETON.

---

### EARL OF BUCHAN TO BRYAN, EIGHTH LORD FAIRFAX.

DRYBURGH ABBEY, November 22, 1798.

My good Lord:

It is proper for me to mention that in consequence of a request notified to me by desire of my Brother of Sergeants Inn that the introductory letter of my truly respectable kinsman,

---

chased by the countess, and turned into a house of worship. Lady Erskine died at Spa-Fields October 5, 1804.

General Washington, which your Lordship handed to me by Lady Anne my sister, should be sent to him for corroboration of your proof of propinquity in Virginia, I did on the 7$^{th}$ of November transmit the said letter to my Brother of which I am sure he will make the best use.

It will give me great pleasure to hear of your health being restored, which the access you can now have to the best regimen in London will offer humanly speaking the greatest probability. I am my good Lord, with my cordial esteem to General Washington when you write to that excellent person.

Your L'dships most assured friend<br>
and humble servt<br>
BUCHAN.

---

LADY ERSKINE TO HON. AND REV. LORD FAIRFAX.

My Good Lord:

I feared from my not seeing you that you was indisposed, and fully intended sending to enquire after your Lordship, so fully that I had given directions to my servant to go tho' I was myself so much indisposed as to be unable to write, at least with ease. I am thank God better, but except a few hours on the morning of my niece's marriage I have not been out of the house since I saw you. I hope you will on no account set out for the North till you are quite recovered. A relapse is in general worse than a first attack. Remember my good Lord, that 'He that believeth shall not make haste.' I am sincerely interested for your welfare and therefore give you this friendly caution. I received a letter this morning from my brother, Lord Buchan, which informs me of the safe arrival of the young couple at Dryburgh Abbey. My brother Thomas has likewise received an account of his son's safe arrival in America, I think at Baltimore. He was in good health and spirits, and said he thought of proceeding in a few days to Philadelphia.[1] I hope the fever is not there, but the Lord can alike preserve in all places. I still hope I shall see you

---

[1] David Montagu son of Lord Erskine, married in 1800 Fanny, daughter of General Cadwallader of Philadelphia, Pa. In 1806 he was a member of parliament, and then minister to the United States. He returned to England in 1809.

before you leave London, but not at the risk of health. * * * * I beg to subscribe myself with sincere regard.

 Your Lordships obliged friend
  and faithful humble servant
    A. A. ERSKINE.

Spa-Fields,
 Dec. 3, 1798.

---

JAMES CHALMER BARRISTER TO BRYAN, LORD FAIRFAX.

ABINGDON STREET, 11 January, 1799.

My Lord:

I had the honour of your letter of the 7$^{th}$ instant and in consequence wrote to Dr Fairfax of Leeds Castle from whom I have a return this day. He says his sight is very bad, and he is otherwise ill, his letter scarcely legible shows it. He says he knew your father, and your brother George, but in what way your father was connected with the last Lord Fairfax he is perfectly ignorant. His evidence can therefore serve us very little. Your eldest brother having administered to the personal

estate of your Uncle Henry, is material as showing he died without issue, and perhaps more may be made out by it when examined * * * * matters now I think, come just to the point, of making out that William your father, was the second son of Henry, the second son of Henry Lord Fairfax who married Miss Barwick. * * *
I am my Lord. Your Lop's

Most obed't servt<br>
JA. CHALMER.

---

THOMAS, LORD ERSKINE TO BRYAN, LORD FAIRFAX.

My dear Lord:

I saw the Chancellor with Mr Chalmer immediately after I left you, and he manifests the most liberal disposition towards you and has no doubt of your right of succession. * * * As to the expense of Council, it is out of the question, as I will be your Council, and if either your health and your natural anxieties lead you to wish to return directly to America, I will take care that your title shall be secured to you as effectually as if you was on the spot  \*  \*  \* I am your Lordship's very sincere

and obed't serv't<br>T. ERSKINE.

---

EARL OF BUCHAN TO BRYAN, LORD FAIRFAX.

DRYBURGH ABBEY, January 14th, 1799.

My Lord:

I have had great satisfaction in considering your simple and unaffected delineation of that part of the worthy General Washington's conduct and character, which has been personally known to your Lordship, and which will remain among my papers as a very amiable and authentic document. I have greatly revered the character of our illustrious kinsman ever since the year 1766 when I became first acquainted with it, and it gives me pleasure to think that the congeniality of our sentiments, has procured for me, some little share of his esteem. Captain Erskine who is here continues to speak of your Lordship with great respect and interest in your welfare, as connected with your own merit, and the wishes of our family for your happiness and desires to be so mentioned in this letter to your Lordship.

There is a most worthy and respectable clergyman Mr Wyvill of Burton Hall near Bedale in Yorkshire to whom as a friend of mine I have written that your Lo'p and he were to become acquainted. \* \* \*
My nephew David, eldest son of my brother Thomas would I rather think be at Mount Vernon, or with the General wherever he happened then to be, about the middle of November. He had letters from me to the General, and was to depend upon him for general instructions with regard to his proposed tour in the United States. It was a happy circumstance that the malignant fever had ceased before my nephew's arrival in America, and I am now in daily expectation of receiving letters from him relating to the progress he has made, in the objects of his expedition.

I gave him few letters, but they were all to good and effective men, better than scores of those that are usually sought for and obtained by common travellers.

All at this Abbey join in good wishes to your Lordship and I remain with much esteem.

Your Lordships affectionate kinsman
& obed't humble servt
BUCHAN.

LADY ERSKINE TO BRYAN, LORD FAIRFAX.

My Good Lord:

My young friend Mr Start returned full of gratitude to your Lordship, for your very kind attention to him, and waits on you to-day with much pleasure. I make him the bearer of this to ask if you will dine and spend the day with me to morrow. Doctor Haweis[1] preaches in the morning and Doctor Ford in the evening.

Next Wednesday, the meeting of the Missionary Society begins, and your Lordship perhaps would wish to attend the preachings at the various places, and if so Mr Start shall attend you, if it should meet wishes: but of this we shall have an opportunity of better settling

[1] Thomas Haweis born in 1734. Graduated at Cambridge. Chaplain of Countess of Huntington, and in charge of her Theological Seminary. He died in 1820.

when I have the pleasure of seeing you tomorrow. I am with much regard

Your Lordships obliged friend

& humble servant

A. A. ERSKINE.

Spa-Fields,
May 4th, 1799.

---

ISABELLA, COUNTESS GLENCAIRN [1] TO BRYAN, LORD FAIRFAX.

My Lord:

Mr Start whom I consider to be a very excellent and deserving Minister of Truth, having in the course of mentioning your Lordship's goodness towards him, conveyed in the flattering distinction of obtaining your countenance in America to enjoy which his whole mind seems disposed, informed me you were shortly to leave this kingdom.

I have to request that unless you should be induced to take Margate in the way to embarkation, I shall have no opportunity of assuring

---

[1] Lady Isabella Erskine, sister of Lady Ann, first married a Mr. Hamilton, and after his death in 1785 became the wife of John the 15th Earl of Glencairn, who was first an officer of dragoons, then a minister of the church of England.

you of the respect and consideration which your character demands. If you should make such a plan convenient, it would afford me great satisfaction to make Updown a stage for your Lordship's accommodation, and I have the honor to remain My Lord

Your most obed't serv't<br>
I. GLENCAIRN.

UPDOWN, May 29th, 1799.

---

REV. JOHN NEWTON TO THE RIGHT HON. AND REV. LORD FAIRFAX.

My dear Lord:

I hear you are about returning to America, but how near to your departure, I know not. If you are in London after the 15th September, I shall hope to express my respects and best wishes to your Lordship *viva voce*. I mean to be in town if the Lord pleases on the 10th or 11th, but after so long an absence, I expect to be much engaged for a few days but hope to be at home all day on Saturday the 14.

But for fear I should not have the pleasure of seeing you before you embark, I must in this way express my regard; and assure you of a place in my frequent remembrance and prayers. May the Lord who brought you safely across the Atlantic, return you safely to your family and friends. The winds and the waves obey Him, and under his care the sea is no less safe than the land. May new causes of praise and thanksgiving meet you on your arrival. I shall pray, that if it is best for you, your health may be established; if not that all your indispositions may be sanctified; so that if the outward tabernacle droops, your soul may thrive, grow in grace, peace and comfort. A favorite Author of mine (the late Mr Adam[1] of Winteringham) has advanced a maxim, which though it may sound strange, I believe to be well founded. He says 'Health is the greatest temporal blessing we can receive, except sickness.' I believe the number of those who profit by sickness, may be equal to the number of those who make a due improvement of health and good spirits. If the

---

[1] Thomas Adam born at Leeds in 1701, was for fifty-eight years, Rector of Winteringham, Lincolnshire. No offer of preferment could induce him to relinquish his charge. He died in 1784, and was the author of several religious works.

Lord afflicts those who love him, it is for their good. If they are in heaviness He sees there is a need-be for it. When horses are high-fed and have little exercise, they soon grow restive. Thus it is said "when Jeshurun waxed fat he kicked." Ah! we knew not, how we should have kicked, nor whether we should have run, if the Lord had not in mercy fed us at times upon the spare diet of affliction!

If I miss you this time, I expect to see you no more upon earth, but I trust we shall meet in a better world. There we shall look back by a clearer light upon all the way by which the Lord led us in this wilderness, and then I believe we shall be sensible that some of our sharpest trials while upon earth, deserve to be ranked amongst our greatest mercies.

What cause, my Lord have we to be thankful for a good hope thro' grace. How does it add to the relish of all our temporal comforts, and alleviate the burden of our troubles. And it is a good hope if simply founded upon the person, love, atonement, and mediation of Jesus. He is set forth to be the brazen serpent to the wounded Israelites, and the invitation is general, unclogged, with no exceptions or conditions, it is only *Look and live.*

May the Lord give you a lively sense of the truth of his declaration, 'Him that cometh I will *in no wise* cast out,' and that 'He is able, willing, and determined to save *to the uttermost,* those who thus come to God by him.'

I trust your Lordship will sometimes think of me at the throne of Grace.

I am my Lord<br>Your affectionate and obliged<br>JOHN NEWTON.[1]

SOUTHAMPTON, the 20 August, 1799,
   at Walter Taylor's, Esq.

---

[1] Rev. John Newton was born in London 1725, and after going to sea at an early age with his father, accompanied him to York Fort, when he became governor of the Hudson's Bay Company.

After his father's death in 1750, he was engaged in the African slave trade. With a change of views as to the chief end of life, being a fine scholar, he applied for ordination to the ministry, and was ordained in 1766, by the Bishop of Lincoln, and for sixteen years was curate of Olney in Buckinghamshire, and there was the friend of the poet Cowper. In 1779 he removed to London and their died in 1807, at the age of eighty-five years. "One there is above all others," "Sometimes a light surprises," "How sweet the name of Jesus sounds," and many other hymns now incorporated in the hymnology of the church are his compositions.

# DESCENDANTS O

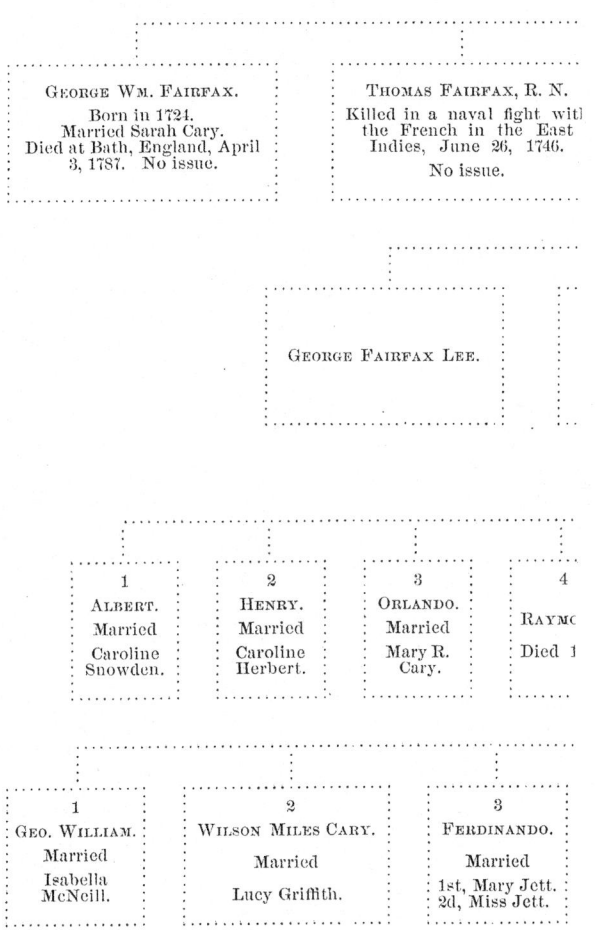

WILLIAM FAIRFAX OF BELVOIR, VIRGINIA, UNITED STATES OF AMERICA.

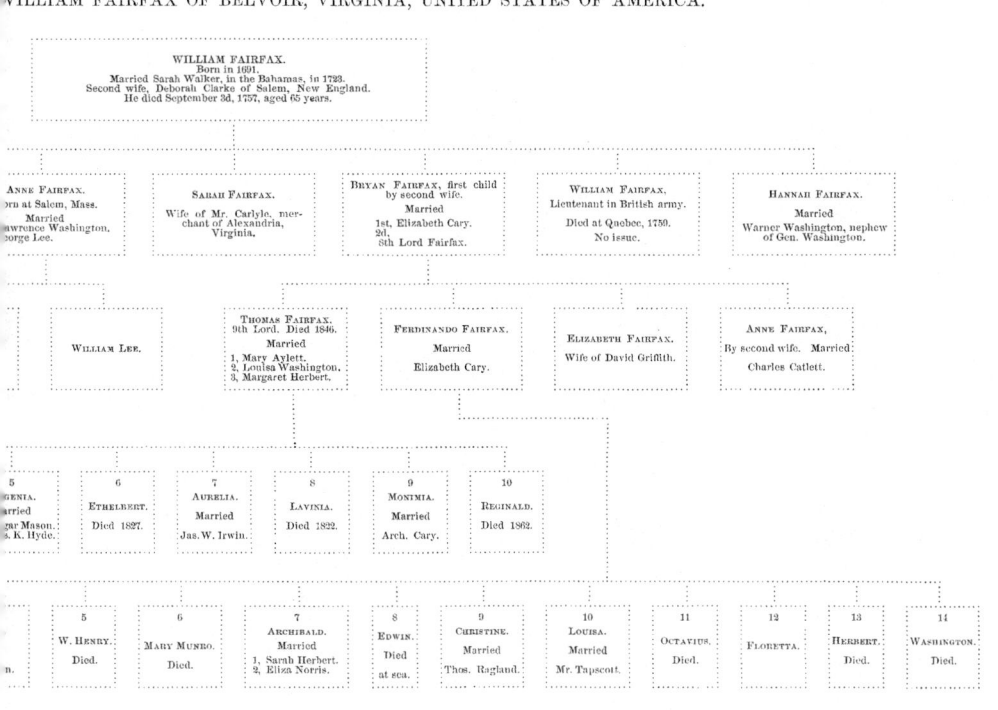

# ADDITIONAL NOTES.

### *Page* 17, *Marriage Notice.*

In Lysons, London, is the following, taken from the parish register of Hackney:

"Thomas Fairfax, Esq., married to Ann, daughter to Rt. Hon. Lord Vere, June 20, 1637."

### *Page* 22, *Thomas, Third Lord Fairfax.*

In the chapel of Bilbrough, erected in the fifteenth century, is the monument to Thomas, Third Lord Fairfax, and wife with this inscription:

"Here lye the bodyes of the Right Hon'ble Thomas, Lord Fairfax of Denton, Baron of Cameron, who dyed November, y$^e$ xii, 1671, in the 60th yeare of his age.

And of Anne, his wife, daughter and co-heir of Horatio, Lord Vere, Baron of Tilbury. They had issue Mary, Duchess of Buckingham, and Elizabeth.

"The memory of the past is blessed."

Elizabeth died in early youth.

### *Page* 52, *Thomas Fairfax, R. N.*

The following inscription was prepared by Hon. Wm. Fairfax of Belvoir, Va., a few hours after receiving the news that his son Thomas had been killed in battle:

"To the memory of Mr. Thomas Fairfax, second son of William Fairfax, Esquire, who died fighting in his country's cause, on board the Harwich ship of war in an engagement with Monsieur Bourdenaye, commander of a French squadron on the Indian coast, the 26th day of June, 1746, and in the twenty-first year of his age; beloved of his commander Captain Carteret, and highly favored by his friend, Commodore Barnet, for his politeness of manners.

"He was a comely personage; of undoubted bravery; skilled in the theory of the profession; excelled by few as a naval draughtsman; and gave early promises by a pregnant genius and diligent application of a consummate officer for the service of his country. But the wisdom of Heaven is inscrutable, human life is ever in the hands of its author; and while the good and brave are always ready for death, resignation becomes their surviving friends. Convinced of this duty, yet subdued by the sentiments of a tender parent, the tablet was inscribed and dedicated by his sorrowful father.

> "May Britain, all thy sons like him behave;
> Like him be virtuous and like him be brave;
> Thy fiercest foes undaunted he withstood,
> And perished fighting for his country's good."

---

*Page* 79, *Thomas Brian Martin, Esq.*

"In the year 1751, Thomas Martin Esq., second son of [Lord Fairfax's] sister Frances, come over to Virginia to live with his lordship; and a circumstance happened a few years after his arrival, too characteristic of Lord Fairfax not to be recorded. After General Braddock's defeat in the year 1755, the Indians in the interest of the French, committed the most dreadful massacres.   *   *   *

Every planter of name or reputation became an object of their insidious designs, and as Lord Fairfax had been pointed out to them as a captain or chief of great renown, the possession of his scalp, they would have regarded as a trophy of inestimable value. With this view they made daily inroads into the vicinage of Greenway Court.   *   * In this crisis of danger his lordship importuned by his friends to retire to the inner settlements, is said to have addressed his nephew in the following manner:

"Colonel Martin, the danger we are exposed to may possibly excite in your mind anxiety. If so I am ready to take any step that you may judge expedient for our common safety. I myself am an old man, and it is of little importance whether I fall by the tomahawk of an Indian or by disease and old age; but you are young. I will therefore submit it to you, whether we shall remain where we are.   *   *   * If we remain it is possible that we may both fall victims; if we retire the whole district will immediately break up, and all the trouble to settle this fine country will be frustrated, and the occasion perhaps, irrecoverably lost.

"Col. Martin after a short deliberation determined to remain, and the danger gradually diminished and at length entirely disappeared." — *Burnaby's Travels, p.* 165.

*Page 92, Hon. William Fairfax.*

The Rev. Dr. Burnaby, Archdeacon of Liecester, who in 1760 was a guest of Washington at Mt. Vernon, says:

" Mr. Willliam Fairfax was a gentleman of very fine accomplishments, and general good character. He was a kind husband, an indulgent parent, a faithful friend, a sincere Christian, and was eminently distinguished for his private and public virtues. Through the interest of his relations, Brian and Ferdinando Fairfax who lived in London, and of whom the former was a commissioner of the excise, he had been appointed collector of the customs of South Potomac, and one of his majesty's council, of which, in process of time, he became president."

Bryan Fairfax was commissioner of customs at London from 1723 to 1748.

---

## *Page* 153, *George William Fairfax.*

" In the year 1773, some estates in Yorkshire having devolved to him by the death of Henry, his father's eldest brother, he found it necessary to go to England to take possession of them. So critical was his arrival, that he passed in the River Thames the ill omened tea, which eventually occasioned the separation of the American colonies from the mother-country. During the ten years' contest, the consequences of which Mr. Fairfax early saw and lamented, his estates in Virginia were sequestered, and he received no remittances from his extensive property. This induced him to remove out of Yorkshire, to lay down his carriages, and to retire to Bath, where he lived in a private but genteel manner, and confined his expenses so much within the income of his English estate, that he was able occasionally to lend large sums to the government agent, for the use and benefit of the American prisoners. He died at Bath on the 3d of April, 1787, in the sixty-third year of his age, and was buried in Writhlington church, in the county of Somerset, a few miles distant from that city. He left a widow, a very amiable lady. * * * Having no issue, he bequeathed his Virginian estates to Ferdinando, the second son of his half-brother Brian, the present Lord Fairfax."— *Burnaby's Travels.*

In his will General Washington was mentioned as an executor.

---

*Page* 165, *Lord Fairfax of Greenway Court, Va.*

Archdeacon Burnaby says: "Lord Fairfax, though possessed of innumerable good qualities, had some few singularities of character. \* \* \* \* Early in life he had formed an attachment to a young lady of quality; and matters had proceeded so far, as to induce him to provide carriages, clothes, servants and other necessary appendages for such an occasion. Unfortunately, or rather let me say fortunately, before the contract was sealed, a more advantageous or dazzling offer was made to the lady, and she preferred the higher honor of being a duchess, to the inferior station of a baroness. This disappointment is thought to have made a deep impression upon Lord Fairfax's mind; and to have had no inconsiderable share in determining him to retire from the world and to settle in the wild and at that time almost uninhabited forests of North America. It is thought also to have excited in him a general dislike of the sex, in whose company, unless he was particularly acquainted with the parties, it is said he was reserved, and under evident constraint and embarassment. But I was present, when upon a visit of ceremony to Lieutenant Governor Fauquier, who had arrived from England he was introduced to his lady, and nothing of the kind appeared to justify the observation. He remained at the palace three or four days; and during that time his behavior was courteous, polite and becoming a man of fashion. \* \* \* He had lived many years retired from the world, in a remote wilderness, sequestered from all polished society; and perhaps might not feel himself at ease when he came into large parties of ladies; but he had not forgot those accomplished manners which he had acquired in his early youth, at Leeds castle, at the University and in the army. His motive for settling in America was of the most noble and heroic kind. It was always as he declared, to settle and cultivate that beautiful and immense tract of which he was the proprietor; and in this he succeeded beyond his most sanguine expectations, for the Northern Neck was better peopled, better cultivated, and more improved than any other part of the dominion of Virginia. Lord Fairfax lived to extreme old age at Greenway Court, universally beloved, and died as universally lamented in January or February, 1782, in the 92d year of his age. He was buried, I believe, at Winchester. He bequeathed Greenway Court to his nephew, Colonel Martin, who has since constantly resided there; and his barony descended to his only surviving brother, Robert Fairfax, to whom he had before consigned Leeds castle, and his other English estates."

# MISCELLANEOUS PAPERS.

#### APPENDIX A.

*Extract of a singular and very expressive letter from an officer to his colonel, concerning the late battle where Capt. Jones lost his life, who commanded a fort on the Mohawk river with 60 men.*

They have used me very ill about the last Battle. They have condemned me tho' I did better than I expected. I declare upon my honor that tho' I run yet it was always in company. I ran three times which is a proof that I rallied twice which is more than many others can say, and it is a great thing for a raw soldier to rally twice that had never been in fight before. I wish to have no more of it if this is all I am to get. I declare upon my honor that I fired that day at least six times when in the afternoon several muskets were pickt up that were never fired at all. A man I think may speak in his own praise when he is condemned. The Battle was in confusion almost from first to last, owing to several parties coming in during the time of action. I'll tell you Sir how it was.

Early in the morning an Indian was seen from the Fort, and it was either not believed or not minded. About 10 o'clock two Indians were seen crossing from the East side of the River about half a mile above the Fort which you know lies on the West side. Cap. Jones went out immediately with 40 men tho' several looked upon it as a decoy.

He said he would have sent me but he was afraid I might be too rash and expose his men. Poor man if he had known my heart at that time he would not have thought so. I was always afraid in a thunder Gust when I did not look for more than one Bullet to fall near me this made me think how I could stand up against hundreds, and nothing but the Love of my country could have brought me into these wild Woods. Between the Fort and where the two Indians crossed there is a large stream of water which was then full with the rains. When we came to the stream for I was with him, we went up it and found that the Indians by their tracks had crossed over to our side, which they need not have done, as their company was lodged on the top of a mountain on the other side two miles off, which shows that they tried to draw us into a trap. They dropt meal to make their track plainer. Capt. Jones followed and crossed the River on a large tree just above a Mill Pond, and went up the mountain; and near the top we were fired upon from a Heap of Rocks, and Capt. Jones being foremost was shot down at the first fire. However his men stood and fought behind the trees, and tried to shout and holloo like the Indians, almost immediately a long string of Indians run down the mountain about 50

APPENDIX. 217

yards above us and got down in the Bottom to cut us off from the tree across the Run. So they had us between two fires. And you may be sure it is no trifling thing for a man to stand and load his gun when he sees an Indian about to fire at him.

Now soon after Capt Jones left the Fort the voluntiers from New York arrived with two Captains and 120 men. And they had just got in when the action began. Of course they immediately set off with great eagerness half run, half walk, for it was a cloudy day and the firing was heard very plainly. When they got near the place, the two Captains having Guides divided their men that they might come the better into Fight. Capt. Harris was to cross at the tree above, and Capt. Bailey at the Dam below. But unluckly the Battle was just then over, we had given way, and run down the side of the mountain and along the Bottom, and were all crossing at the mill dam just as Capt. Bailey came to it. The water was running over half leg deep, and no man in his sober sense would have crossed it; but what will not flying troops do? About this time the Indian Chiefs 'tis supposed on the mountain seeing Capt. Harris and his men coming up to the tree gave three war whoops and called back their people that pursued. This enabled Capt. Bailey to carry over about twenty of his men with some of ours that had been engaged, for he said he was bound to go over and support those that went to cross above — and he went up the mountain and along the Ridge with five men, the rest lagged behind, one stopt to cut a new ramrod, pretending the old one was too light; another sat down to pick his flint and so on; however, most of them got on along the side of the mountain so as to shoot at a distance and keep up the fight on that side. But this was not all. Ten waggons with an escort of twenty men arrived also at the Fort about a quarter of an hour after the New Yorkers were gone and hearing the shouting and screaming they were also intent to go; and the waggoners mounted their horses and with the escort set out to join — these coming up just as Capt. Harris, who had crossed the tree and engaged the Indians, was driven back again with some of his men, tho' others of them in moving about during the fight had got so much below it that they could not cross it again, and therefore they joined Bailey's on the mountain's side and continued the fight. The foremost waggoner meeting Capt. Harris and his men, called out, Why — we are coming to help you — Come along, I'll show you a Ford a little higher up. Several of these went to the Ford and by that means engaged on that side; yet a few of these also run away. There is one thing more which was the finishing stroke. So many of the runaways had got back to the Fort that the officer who was left there suffered his men at last also to go, who had been impatient to join, and who took with them some of their brother soldiers that had been in the first action, and had come down from the dam. These came in with fresh threats, and were of singular service, as the stoutest lungs commonly carry the day when there is a heart to use them. As soon as they came in, the Indians seemed discouraged at so many Reinforcements their fire slackened, and they broke ground and run and were obliged to cross track that our people had so often crossed that day. It does not appear that more than sixty or seventy of our men were ever engaged at one time, tho' we had near 240 within hearing.

When the Indians gave way there was a general shout, and it put new life into all, and engaged us the more eagerly in the chase. As this letter was begun for the sake of my own Vindication you will expect me to tell in a more particular manner how I was employed that day. And I will tell you the truth, and defy any man to contradict it. I went out with Capt. Jones, and fought and retreated with his men; and when we came to the dam Capt. Bailey wanted me to return which I had no mind to do, I said, "It is unreasonable to expect that a man just escaped from battle should have as much heart to return over such a dangerous place and that in the face of an Enemy as he that is just entering into it. Do you go over with your men if you like it and I'll go and join Capt. Harris on this side." So we parted. He went over with as many as he could get to follow him and I went up the Run to the tree with six of my men and two of the volunteers. I joined Capt. Harris and retreated when he did and went up to the Ford with him and the others; and when all who about me and near me to the ——— of twenty ran away, I ran too, and never joined him again till the Indians gave way which was within twenty minutes when they running by us we joined in with those that pursued them. This accounts for my saying that I run three times and rallied twice, and yet was in at the chase — for I had the conscience to call that a Rally, because the Indians came running by us and we followed as soon as we had company — I was at that time with another Officer sitting on the side of a mountain taking breath after we had been trying to bring some back to the field of Battle. We killed or rather found killed in a dispersed manner eight Indians in all, and we lost twelve men, besides twenty wounded. From first to last, the fight lasted near three hours, for ——— was full five miles long and we had a much greater number in the chase than we ever had collected before. The stragglers came in from all parts.

You will see from this statement that my acquittal from Blame or not will depend upon what passed at the Dam, which caused Capt. Bailey to say such hard things of me as he has. However, I will do him the justice to say that the success of the Battle was chiefly owing to him, and that he is highly to be praised for going along the Ridge with only five men and trying to coax on the others in order to support his Brother officer, without this the Battle would have been totally lost and many more killed. The waggoners deserve the next praise — and Capt. Harris the next and he is not to be blamed, or who would be an Officer. Besides this — I think a man that strives against his natural fears shows more virtue than he who acts bravely without fear. I saw an Instance of this in the late Action: a worthy man whom I know, when we crossed the Ford and engaged, looked as pale as ashes, his hands and knees trembled and yet he tried to fight, did put up the gun to his face and fired — soon after when some Indians came pressing in very close and fired, he seemed to fall thro' fear, for he was close by me, yet he did not run nor attempt it. I left him sitting when I gave way the last time. And yet this man was in at the chase and not among the Hindmost.

## APPENDIX B.

### Tithables in Virginia, October, 1748.

| | | | |
|---|---|---|---|
| Accomack, | 2353 | Lunenburg, | 1519 |
| Albemarle, | 1725 | Middlesex, | 1400 |
| Amelia, | 2383 | Nansemond, | 2153 |
| Augusta, | 1423 | New Kent, | 1610 |
| Brunswick, | 1765 | Norfolk, | 2190 |
| Caroline, | 3551 | Northampton, | 1529 |
| Charles City, | 1506 | Northumberland, | 2176 |
| Elizabeth City, | 1070 | Orange, | 2679 |
| Essex, | 2610 | Princess Ann, | 1559 |
| Fairfax, | 1586 | Prince George, | 3190 |
| Frederick, | 1581 | Prince William, | 2222 |
| Gloucester, | 4307 | Richmond, | 1837 |
| Goochland, | 2773 | Spotsylvania, | 1782 |
| Hanover, | 3108 | Stafford, | 1811 |
| Henrico, | 2979 | Surry, | 3367 |
| James City, | 1543 | Warwick, | 818 |
| Isle of Wight, | 3244 | Westmoreland, | 2471 |
| King George, | 1744 | York, | 2054 |
| King & Queen, | 2899 | | |
| King William, | 2392 | Total in 1748, | 85919 |
| Lancaster, | 1538 | Total October 1752, | 95000 |
| Louisa, | 1519 | | |

## APPENDIX C.

### Tithables in Virginia in 1757.

| COUNTIES. | WHITES. | BLACKS. | TOTAL. |
|---|---|---|---|
| Accomack, | 1506 | 1135 | 2641 |
| Amelia, | 1251 | 1652 | 2903 |
| Albemarle, | 1344 | 1747 | 3091 |
| Augusta, | 2273 | 40 | 2303 |
| Brunswick, | 1299 | 976 | 2275 |
| Bedford, | 357 | 143 | 500 |
| Charles City, | 537 | 1058 | 1595 |
| Caroline, | 1208 | 2674 | 3882 |
| Chesterfield, | 841 | 1198 | 2039 |
| Culpepper, | 1221 | 1217 | 2438 |
| Cumberland, | 704 | 1394 | 2098 |
| Dinwiddie, | 787 | 1175 | 1962 |
| Elizabeth City, | 316 | 812 | 1128 |
| Essex, | 889 | 1711 | 2600 |
| Fairfax, | 1312 | 921 | 2233 |
| Frederick, | 2173 | 340 | 2513 |
| Gloucester, | 1137 | 3284 | 4421 |
| Goochland, | 569 | 935 | 1504 |
| Henrico, | 529 | 898 | 1427 |
| Hanover, | 1169 | 2621 | 3790 |
| Hampshire, | 558 | 12 | 570 |
| Halifax, | 629 | 141 | 770 |
| James City, | 394 | 1254 | 1648 |
| Isle of Wight, | 810 | 966 | 1776 |
| King & Queen, | 944 | 2103 | 3047 |
| King William, | 702 | 1834 | 2536 |
| King George, | 702 | 1068 | 1788 |
| Lancaster, | 486 | 1124 | 1610 |
| Louisa, | 655 | 1452 | 2107 |
| Lunenburg, | 1209 | 983 | 2192 |
| Middlesex, | 371 | 1056 | 1427 |
| Norfolk, | 1132 | 1408 | 2540 |
| Nansemond, | 989 | 1264 | 2253 |
| Northampton, | 609 | 902 | 1511 |
| New Kent, | 465 | 1209 | 1674 |
| Northumberland, | 980 | 1434 | 2414 |
| Orange, | 627 | 1016 | 1643 |
| Princess Ann, | 840 | 880 | 1720 |
| Prince George, | 650 | 1138 | 1788 |
| Prince William, | 1384 | 1414 | 2798 |
| Prince Edward, | 416 | 410 | 826 |
| Richmond, | 716 | 1235 | 1996 |

## Tithables in Virginia in 1757 — continued.

| COUNTIES. | WHITES. | BLACKS. | TOTAL. |
|---|---|---|---|
| Surry, | 587 | 1006 | 1593 |
| Stafford, | 889 | 1126 | 2015 |
| Spotsylvania, | 665 | 1468 | 2133 |
| Southampton, | 973 | 1036 | 2009 |
| Sussex, | 778 | 1388 | 2166 |
| Westmoreland, | 944 | 1588 | 2532 |
| Warwick, | 181 | 665 | 846 |
| York, | 562 | 1567 | 2129 |
| Total 50, | 44214 | 58292 | 103556 |

## APPENDIX D.

*Tobacco exported from Virginia from 1745 until 1750.*

| EXPORTS. | 1745 | 1746 | 1747 | 1748 | 1749 |
|---|---|---|---|---|---|
| Upper District of James River,.... | 10991 | 10799 | 9355 | 12489 | 11509 |
| Lower District of James River,.... | 1381 | 1372 | 1718 | 3170 | 3150 |
| York River,..................... | 11118 | 11015 | 12895 | 11089 | 10970 |
| Rappahannock,.................. | 12332 | 10745 | 12132 | 13052 | 15012 |
| South Potomac,................. | 6659 | 6311 | 5704 | 6983 | 7346 |
| Hhds.,............... | 42481 | 40242 | 41804 | 46783 | 47987 |

*Tobacco exported from 1750 until 1755.*

| EXPORTS. | 1750 | 1751 | 1752 | 1753 | 1754 |
|---|---|---|---|---|---|
| Upper District of James River,.... | 12974 | 10858 | 13530 | 18830 | 13900 |
| Lower District of James River,.... | 2218 | 2525 | 1423 | 2113 | 1181 |
| York River,..................... | 13802 | 12054 | 12623 | 15127 | 14878 |
| Rappahannock,.................. | 14331 | 13553 | 14299 | 16815 | 13512 |
| South Potomac,................. | 5242 | 7713 | 6505 | 6959 | 7332 |
| Accomack,...................... |  |  |  | 3 |  |
| Hhds.,............... | 48567 | 46703 | 48380 | 59847 | 50803 |

*Exports of 1755, 1756.*

| EXPORTS. | 1755 | 1756 |
|---|---|---|
| Upper District of James River,......... | 13739 | 7262 |
| Lower District of James River,......... | 918 | 1096 |
| York River,.......................... | 15344 | 6918 |
| Rappahannock,....................... | 11963 | 8531 |
| South Potomac,...................... | 5723 | 4645 |
| Accomack 11 barrels.................. |  |  |
| Hhds., ......................... | 47687 | 28452 |

# INDEX.

Adam, Rev. Thomas, sketch of, 206.
Addison, Anthony, 167: John, surveyor-general of Maryland, 167:
  Rev. Henry, sketch of, 167; portrait of, 168.
Addison's tragedy of Cato, 106, 107.
Alexandria, Va., formerly Bell Haven, 89: Presbyterian minister
  of, 139.
Ambler, Edward, 102: H., mantua maker, 124: Richard, 113, 157.
Apple grafts, 99.
Athawes, Edmund, 97, 113: Samuel, 120, 150, 157, 174.

Barwick, Sir Robert, 23, 56: Ursula, 25; letter to her son, 25.
Bassett, William, 136.
Baylis, Mr., 100.
Baylor, John, visits Scotland, 171, 172; sketch of, 171.
Belvoir, seat of G. W. Fairfax, 83, 153; described by Washington,
  180.
Bishop of London, 128.
Blacklock, Rev. Dr., 159.
Bladen, Col, Martin, 64, 65, 67; Mary wife of, 71: Nathaniel, bar-
  rister, 29.
Boarding school proposed, 152.
Boston Port Bill, 148, 149.
Boucher, Rev. Jonathan, letter of, 167; sketch of, 169.
Braddock, General, 89.
Brodeau, Mrs., school of, 152.
Buchan, Earl, sketch of, 191; admiration of Washington, 201.
Buckskins, nickname of frontiersmen, 134.
Bullitt, Capt., at Fort Duquesne, 105.
Bunker Hill battle, 160.
Burk, error in History of Virginia, 47.
Burnaby, Archdeacon, biographical sketches, 209, 214.
Burwell, Carter, 152.
Byng, Admiral John, 86: Sir G., notice of, 62.

Campbell, error in History of Virginia, 47: Matthew, 139.
Carter family, 113: Charles, 113; Joseph, 99: Robert, 113.
Cary, Colonel, sketch of, 115; objects to daughter's marriage, 102:
    Elizabeth, wife of Rev. Bryan Fairfax, 108: Mary, early love
    of Washington, 101; letter from Washington, 103: Sarah,
    wife of George W. Fairfax, 81, 95, 119.
Cheeseman, Captain, 85.
Chester, Captain, 84.
Clapham, Dorothy, 86: H., 85: Jo of Annapolis, 121, 167: Josiah
    of Leesburg, 121: Rev. Mr., chaplain 4th Lord Fairfax, 37.
Clargis, Sir Thomas, 19.
Clarke, Deborah, 48.
Clubs, Jockey, 144.
Cocke, Captain, 82, 108.
Constable, Sir Wm, 10, 11.
Cooling, Captain, 78.
Corbin family, 136: Frank, educated in England, 137, 144, 147:
    Richard, obtains Washington's commission, 136.
Croft, Stephen, on American troubles, 162.
Cromwell, Oliver, 3.
Culpepper, Catharine, marries 5th Lord Fairfax, 39.
Custis family, 147: Jno. Parke, 147; Martha 110.

Danby, Earl of, 29.
Dawson, Rev. Thomas, 127.
Delicia, ship, 69, 74.
Dent, Mr., 117.
Denton Hall, seat of General Lord Fairfax, 37.
Dinwiddie, Governor, 80.
Dulany, Daniel, 167.
Dunbar, Colonel, 80.
Dundas, Lady, 159.
Dunmore, Gov., leaves Williamsburg, 158; threatens Hampton, 171.
Dunton, John, 44.
Duquesne, fort, 104.

Eden, Captain, Thomas, 135; Robert, Governor of Maryland, 135.
Erskine, David, Earl of Buchan, 191, 196: David Montagu, sketch
    of, 198; visits U. States, 202; marries, 198: Ann Agnes, Lady,
    195, 197, 203; Isabella, Countess of Glencairn, 204: Thomas,
    Lord Chancellor, 193.
Everett, Edward, error in article on Washington, 101.
Eyre, Littleton, 91.

Fairfax, Thomas, *First Lord*, 8 ; children, 9 ; death, 8.
 Ferdinando, *Second Lord*, 9 ; at Marston Moor, 9 ; writes to Lady Vere, 14.
 Thomas, *Third Lord*, 9 ; marriage, 17, 209 ; hero of Naseby, 9 ; visits Charles 2d, 20 ; sickness and death, 21, 22 ; inscription on tomb, 209 ; sketch of, 18.
 Henry, *Fourth Lord*, 28 ; notice of, 28, 37 ; letters of, 34, 36.
 Thomas, *Fifth Lord*, 37 ; notice of, 39 ; letters of, 41.
 Thomas, *Sixth Lord*, 49 ; proprietor of Northen Neck, 49 ; grandson of L'd Culpeper, 77 ; in Virginia, 77 ; death of, 165 ; notice of, 213 ; letters of, 77, 78, 79, 83, 84, 91, 98, 99, 111.
 Robert, *Seventh Lord*, 91 ; visits Virginia, 96 ; at Greenway Court, 134 ; notice of, 214.
 Bryan, *Eight Lord*, 175 ; a neutral, 176 : intimate with Washington, 176 ; enters the sacred ministry, 177 ; visits England, 181 ; at Washington's funeral, 182 ; donation to Bishop Seabury, 186.
Fairfax, Ann, wife of Sheriff Henry, 61, 71 : Anna wife of Lawrence Washington, 52 : Bryan, cousin of 3d Lord, 19, 28 ; brother of Hon William, 63, 69 ; see Eight Lord Fairfax, 175 : Dorothy, wife of Sir W. Constable, 9 ; daughter of 4th Lord Fairfax, 72 ; sister of Hon. William, 86 : Frances, daughter of 4th Lord Fairfax, 34 : George William, Son of Hon William, 51 ; travels with Washington 51 ; writes to Dinwiddie, 80 ; visits England in 1757, 93 ; declines to be a candidate for House of Burgesses, 98 ; visits England again, 117 ; writes to Washington, 123 ; sick in England, 122 ; his mare Moggy, 126 ; visits Scotland, 131 ; Burnaby's sketch of, 212 : Hannah, wife of Warner Washington, 52 : Henry, Rev., father of 4th Lord, 28 ; Sheriff of Yorkshire, 34, 53 ; notes from his father, 34 ; note to his wife, 35 ; notice of, 37 : Henry, son of the sheriff, 47 ; at Lowther school, 54, Isabella, wife of Nath. Bladen, 28 : Mary, wife of Henry Arthington, 13 : Mary, wife of Duke of Buckingham, 17, 18 : Robert, admiral British navy, 61 : Thomas, royal navy, killed in East Indies, 52 ; obituary notice, 209 : William, of Steeton, killed, 23 ; letter from, 23 : William, Pres. of Va. Council, 47 ; attends Lowther school, 48, 54 ; enters navy, 48, 55, 56 ; letters to mother, 62, 64, 69, 74 ; marriage, 48, 74 ; judge at the Bahamas, 74 ; collector of Salem, Mass., 48 ; wife dies, 48, 74 ; marries again, 49 ; moves to Virginia, 49 ; daughter wife of L. Washington, 49 ; Collector for South Potomac, 51 ; death of, 90, 91 sketch of, 211 : William, son of Hon. William, 52 ; Ensign 28th

Fairfax, *continued.*
>British Infantry, 105; fatally wounded at Quebec, 106, 114; General Wolfe's remark to, 106.

Falls Church, 178.
Falls of the Potomac, 183.
Family of Addison, 167; Baylor, 170; Carter, 113; Cary, 115; Clapham, 121, 167; Corbin, 136; Dawson, 127; Fauntleroy, 144; Green, 117; Hoge, 84; Hollingsworth, 100; Lee, 111; Lewis, 79; Mercer, 143; Mc Carty, 80; Neill, 99; Nelson. 115; Nicholas, 138; Norton, 147; Randolph, 164; Shaw, 157; Tayloe, 143; Tucker, 160; Washington, 60.
Fauntleroys, 144.
Fillmore, Sir Edward, 77.
Flood, Dr William, 144.
Ford, Rev Dr., 203.
Fordyce, Captain, 174.
Fothergill, Dr., 152; quaker preacher, 87.

Gale, Colonel, 75.
Gazette, London, 114.
Germantown, Pa., 188.
George 3d, proposed marriage, 122.
Gift, Washington's horse, 126.
Grant, Major, 104.
Great Bridge, fight at, 174.
Green, Rev. Charles, 117, 123, 125.
Greenway Court, residence of 6th Lord Fairfax, 51, 126, 165, 214.
Griffith, Rev. David, bishop elect of Virginia, 177, 180.

Hanbury, Mr. of London, 140, 167.
Harrison, Anna, wife of Sheriff Fairfax, 37, 47, 55; Eleanora wife of H'y Washington, 37.
Hawke, Edward Lord, 123, 165.
Hoge family, 84: John, prisoner in France, 87.
Hollingsworth, Abraham, quaker, 100; family, 100.
Hopkins, Governor of Connecticut., 11.
Horse racing, 144.
Hounds, sent to Virginia, 77.
Huntingdon, Countess, 195.

Indian disturbances in Virginia, 83.
Jockey Clubs, 145.
Johnson, Governor of Maryland, 183; G. W. Barrister, 7.

# INDEX.

Jones, Captain., killed on Mohawk, 215.
Juba, a character in Addison's Cato, 106.

Land Office of Lord Fairfax, 117, 126.
Latimer, Lord, 30.
Lee family, 111: Arthur, member of Continental congress, 112; Francis, 112: F. Lightfoot M. C. 112: George, married widow of L. Washington, 97: Harry, General, 112, 183: Henry, son of Richard, 112: Philip, son of Richard, 112: Philip, Colonel, 112, 153; son of Thomas, 112: Richard, the emigrant, 111; Richard, son of emigrant, 111: Richard, grandson of emigrant, 111: Richard Henry, 112: Thomas, son of Richard, 112: Thomas, grandson of Richard, 112: William, sheriff of London, 112.
Letters of Athawes, Ed., 113; Samuel, 150, 151, 157, 174: Barwick Ursula, 25: Bladen, Mary, 71; Nathaniel, 29: Boucher, Rev. Jonathan, 167: Buchan, Earl of, 191, 197, 201: Campbell, Mathew, 139: Chalmer, James, 199: Clapham, Dorothy, 86; H., 85; Jo., 121; Josias, 183: Corbin, Richard, 147; Croft, Stephen, 160; Erskine, Ann, Lady, 195, 197, 203; Isabella, Lady, 204; Thomas, Lord, 203: Eyre, Littleton, 91: Fairfax, Bryan, brother of 4th Lord, 33: Ferdinando, 2d Lord, 14: George W., 80, 93, 95, 115, 116, 119, 120, 122, 125, 126, 132, 135, 172: Henry, 4th Lord, 34; Sheriff, 35, 53: Robert, 7ht Lord, 134, 164; Admiral 61: Thomas, 5th Lord, 41; 6t, 77, 78, 79, 83, 84, 91, 98, 99, 111: William, Hon., 56, 62, 64, 66, 67, 69, 74, 76; of Steeton, 23: Hawke, Lord, 165: Hoge, John, 87, 88: Lee George, 97: Madison, Bishop of Virginia, 185: Mercer, Geo. F., 146: Middleton. E., 196: Newton, Rev. John, 205: Nicholas, Robt. Carter, 138: Norton, John, 170; J. H., 145, 149: Seabury, Bishop of Connecticut, 186: Shaw, Rev. George, 156: Sherard, Dorothy, 72: Tayloe, John, 143: Thoresby, Ralph, 42: Tucker, Nathaniel, 159, 163: Vere, Lady, 10, 12: Washington, George, 103, 155, 180, 188, 190; Henry, 38; Richard, 57, 59: Widdrington, Lord, 13: Willis, Francis, 137.
Leeds Castle, old oaken chest at, 7.
Lewis, Major, killed at Fort Duquesne, 104.
Lowther, Sir John, 53; School 53.
Lyne, Captain, 171.

Madison, Bishop of Virginia, 185.
Mantua-maker's bill, 124.
Marcia, Addison's, 106.

Martin, Col. T. B., 79, 92, 98, 108, 119, 126, 127, 210.
Mason, Mr., 111, 154.
Mc Carty, family, 80.
Meade, Bishop, on early love of Washington, 101.
Mercer, George, F., proposed Governor of Vandalia, 139.
Mohawk River, fort on, 215.
Monk, General, 18.
Montague, Ralph, 32.
Mosley, Rev. Mr., 130.

Neill, Irish quaker, 99.
Nelson family, 115, 151.
Newton, Rev. John, letter of, 205 ; sketch of, 208.
Nicholas, Captain, 171 ; Robert, Carter, 115, 138,
Northern Neck of Virginia, 128.
Norton, J. H., 146.
Nun Appleton, seat of 3d Lord Fairfax, 21.

Ohio Company, 140.

Page, Rev. Bernard, 180.
Parishes of Virginia elect their pastors, 128.
Pew of Geo. W. Fairfax, 154.
Pohick church, 154.
Potter, Mr., 79.

Randolph, Edmond, 164; John, Attorney General of Virg
    Peyton, 164; William, 164.
Rogers, Governor, Woodes, 68, 69, 74.
Rymer, Rev. Mr., 34.

School, boarding proposed, 152.
Sacheverell, Rev. Dr., 58.
Savage, Doctor, 188.
Seabury, Bishop of Connecticut, 186.
Selim, race horse, 145.
Sharpe, Governor, of Maryland, 83.
Shaw, Rev. George on American troubles, 156.
Skirmish at Hampton, 171.
Sparks, Jared, mistake in Washington genealogy, 61.
Squires, Captain, 171.
Start, Rev. Mr., 204.

INDEX. 233

Stephens, Mr., 99.
Strickland, Sir Walter, 27; William, 27.

Taite, Robert, servant of the Lord Fairfax, 40.
Tayloe family, 143.
Thoresby, Ralph, antiquarian, 44; describes old Fairfax Hall, 44; describes funeral of 4th Lord Fairfax, 37.
Thornton family, 127.
Tithables in Virginia, 222, 223.
Tobacco exported from Virginia, 225.
Tom, Rev. Mr., of Alexandria, 139.
Tucker, Nathaniel, 159, 163; St. George, 163; Henry St. George, 160.

Vandalia, province of proposed, 141.
Vere, Ann, wife of 3d Lord Fairfax, 9; Lady, letters of, 10, 16.
Virginia, assembly dissolved, 148; associators, 149; convention, 149; delegates to Congress, 149.

Walker, Sarah, wife of Hon. W. Fairfax, 48, 71.
Walpole grant, 140.
Washington, genealogy, 60.
    George, on a surveying tour, 51; names an Indian chief, 51; Commissioned as a Colonel, 80; election to the legislature, 98; attachment to Mary Cary, 101; at Fort Duquesne, 110; marries Martha Custis, 110; agent for G. W. Fairfax, 118; contemplated visit to England, 123; letters to, 122, 124; ill health of, 125; his stallion, Gift, 126; confers with Gov. Eden, 135; his first military commission, 137; final money statement to G. W. Fairfax, 155; on Bunker Hill battle, 160; funeral of, 182; letters of, 103, 160, 188, 190.
    Henry, letters of, 37, 38.
    Lawrence, marries Ann Fairfax, 49.
    Martha, 122, 126.
    Richard of London, 55, 57, 60, 123, 125, 131, 132, 133.
    Warner, 52.
Watson, Leonard, 128; Joseph, 139.
West, John, 78, 83.
Widdrington, Lord, 13; Lady, 9.
Williamsburg magazine, 158.
Willis, Francis Jr., 137.
Winthrop, Gov. of Mass., 11.

Wolfe, General, speech to young Fairfax, 106.
Wood, early settler at Winchester, 100.
Wright, Lawrence, of Charter House, London, 11 ; letter of 12.
Wyvill, Rev. Mr., 202.

Yorick, race horse, 144.

---

## ERRATA.

On Page 16, Lord *Widdrington* should read Lord *Fairfax*.
„ „ 21, *New Appleton* „ „ „ *Nun Appleton*.
„ „ 90, *August* 30 „ „ „ *September* 3*d*.

Printed in Dunstable, United Kingdom